HOPE BEYOND THE WRECKAGE

Real Stories from Concord, CA

This book was written for the express purpose of conveying the love and mercy of Jesus Christ. The statements in this book are substantially true; however, names and minor details have been changed to protect people and situations from accusation or incrimination.

All Scripture quotations, unless otherwise noted, are taken from the New International Version Copyright 1973, 1984, 1987 by International Bible Society.

Published in Beaverton, Oregon, by Good Catch Publishing.
www.goodcatchpublishing.com
V1.1

Printed in the United States of America

Table of Contents

DEDICATION

This book is dedicated to all who feel hopeless, trapped, destroyed, addicted or abandoned. No matter the cause of your suffering — the pain of a tragic loss, divorce, rejection, bankruptcy, debilitating medical conditions — we believe you can discover HOPE.

This book is also dedicated to the brave men and women who shared their stories to provide living proof that there is HOPE BEYOND THE WRECKAGE.

ACKNOWLEDGEMENTS

I would like to thank Jeff Kenney for his vision for this book and Missy Kenney for her hard work in making it a reality. To the people of New Hope International, thank you for your boldness and vulnerability in sharing your personal stories.

This book would not have been published without the amazing efforts of our project manager and editor, Samantha Jaquez. Her untiring resolve pushed this project forward and turned it into a stunning victory. Thank you for your great fortitude and diligence. Deep thanks to our incredible editor in chief, Michelle Cuthrell, and executive editor, Jen Genovesi, for all the amazing work they do. I would also like to thank our invaluable proofreader, Melody Davis, for the focus and energy she puts into perfecting our words.

Lastly, I want to extend our gratitude to the creative and very talented Ariana Randle, who designed the beautiful cover for *Hope Beyond the Wreckage: Real Stories from Concord, CA.*

Daren Lindley
President and CEO
Good Catch Publishing

The book you are about to read
is a compilation of authentic life stories.
The facts are true, and the events are real.
These storytellers have dealt with crisis, tragedy, abuse
and neglect and have shared their most private moments,
mess-ups and hang-ups in order for others to learn and
grow from them. In order to protect the identities of those
involved in their pasts, the names and details of some
storytellers have been withheld or changed.

INTRODUCTION

What do you do when life careens out of control? When addiction overtakes you or abuse chains you with fear? Is depression avoidable? Is debt escapable? Can relationships ever be healthy again? Are you destined to live as a prisoner to difficult circumstances or poor choices? Or can the sunlight of HOPE break you free from the trap of the current wreckage that surrounds you?

There is HOPE that your life really can change. It is possible to become a new person. The seven stories you are about to read prove positively that people right here in the Bay Area have stopped dying and started living. Whether you've been beaten by abuse, broken promises, abandoned relationships, shattered dreams or suffocating addictions, the resounding answer is, "Yes! Your life really can change!" The potential to break free from the pain and step into a hopeful future is now in your hands.

Expect inspiration, hope and transformation! As you walk with these real people from our very own city through the pages of this book, you will not only find riveting accounts of their hardships, you will learn the secrets that brought about their breakthroughs. These people are no longer living in the shadows of yesterday; they are thriving with a sense of HOPE, mission and purpose *today*. May these stories inspire you to find hope beyond *your* wreckage.

LIMELIGHT
The Story of Zach
Written by Holly De Herrera

The door squeaked all too loudly when I entered, shadows gray and hunching filled the living room, moonlight filtered around shapes and shadows. It all seemed still and lifeless, even though I knew it wasn't. Darkness lived there with us.

My dad made his presence known in ways that made my skin crawl and my hands itch with a need to strike out. A siren screamed in the background and broke up the quiet a little. I let out a breath, feeling for a moment like I could relax. *No war zone tonight.* No purple-black bruises around my mom's eyes. No yelling or hateful sounds. Just my own breath and my heartbeat, thumping slower. I stood there in the living room letting myself savor the silence. I never knew what I'd come home to. The edges of the chair, the side table, the curtains seemed to smooth as I calmed my breath. *No drama tonight.* No screaming. No blood.

But then from the couch my mom spoke in soft tones, "Son? Is that you?"

"Mom, what are you doing out here?" My voice sounded smaller than I wanted it to. I needed to be the strong one.

"Son." The sickening smell of liquor on her breath filled the air.

"Mom, you've been drinking." My stomach filled with a sour twisting.

"I'm sorry, Zach. So sorry." Her "S's" came out loud and elongated.

Swallowing hard, I said, "Let's get you to bed." I reached down to help her up.

"Nah, just sit with me. I want my boy near." She reached up a hand and pulled on the edge of my shirt.

I lifted her head enough to sit, and then she settled in on my lap, her dark hair looking unkempt and rebellious even in the dark. I smoothed it back away from her forehead, listening as her breathing got deeper and deeper and turned to snoring. Just when it seemed she was out for the night, she woke with a sharp intake of breath, like she had been dreaming and flinching away from some invisible, but very real, blow to the face.

Her eyes looked so wide and white in the muted light. She looked up at me and said, high-pitched and frantic, "That you, son?"

I resumed stroking her frizzy hair. "It's me. You're all right."

"Oh. I thought …"

"I know. But it's not. It's just me."

She rested her head back down. She'd been holding it just above my leg, hovering there. The weight of her pressed on my lap, and before drifting off again, she said, "I love you. So much."

"I love you, too, Mom."

❧❧❧

I was only 9 when I came back from camp and found my mom so bruised and swollen I could hardly recognize her face. She tried to greet me with a smile, but it came out looking ghoulish, like a horror movie character.

"Son. Let's talk."

I set my bag down and backed away. *Who was this person? How could she look this different only days later? And why had Grandma picked me up and taken me to her home instead of Mom getting me and taking us to our place?*

I could tell she had tried her best to look presentable with her clean clothes and her hair smelling fresh and looking all shiny and pulled back in a hair band, but I couldn't get past her face. The way her eye bulged like a fish and the color of her skin, which was no longer a pretty chocolate-brown but yellow-green instead.

"Where is he?" I darted to the back room at Grandma's. Nothing. No sign of my so-called dad. Heat crept up my neck, into my face, pulsed in my ears. "Where?!" I screamed the word without meaning to. This woman who had never hurt a soul now had to bear my wrath.

"Gone," she said, sounding so small and defeated. "Your dad's gone."

"Not my dad. Don't ever say that again."

He had done this to her. I knew it deep inside my stomach, and I hated the man. I knew that if he came around, I'd find a way to shoot him while he slept.

But he was gone, Mom was heartbroken and I could

hardly stand her for that. *How could someone who used you as a punching bag be worth crying a single tear over?* No, he had left, and I was the man of the house now. We'd be all right because what good was he, anyway? He hadn't helped us, only hurt. Only yelled and broken the few things we had that were nice.

"He said I have to sell the house. He wants half the money."

I laughed, but it sounded mean and full of spite. "Like there will be any! But it's worth it to him, I guess, to make us lose our place." His selfishness didn't surprise me, but still I felt I'd been punched in the stomach. *What were we going to do?*

"I have to get a job," she said, "and we need to start packing."

When we got back to our house, it looked like a war zone. The door between the house and garage was streaked with blood and scratch marks, like Mom had been trapped in there and was an animal trying to get out. Broken glass littered the kitchen, the living room, the hall.

I looked over at Mom. Her eyes flicked around the room as if making a mental list of all that needed to happen. All that she now had to do on her own. She turned without a word and left the room, closing her bedroom door behind her. It was like she didn't even see the marks of her suffering. She only saw what she'd lost and the world of hardship to come.

I couldn't see why she would mourn the loss of that man. I shook my head trying to get things straight in my mind. Sure, we'd had our good times. But what stood out to me was how Dad never touched Mom, at least not in a sweet way, never told her she was beautiful or showed her any kind of affection. And he didn't care at all about bringing other women into their bed. The whole thing turned my stomach. Couldn't he see she only wanted to be loved?

I scanned the house and wondered what we were going to do now. How would Mom make enough to feed the three of us, Mom, Leo and me? Maybe I could get a job somewhere. Anywhere. It would be fine. I would take care of things.

I found out years later that even though I was named after Dad, Mom had gotten pregnant by some other man I'd never met. And I wondered if that was maybe why Zach Sr. acted so hateful toward Mom and why he didn't care one bit for Leo and me. So I wasn't a junior like I had thought. I was just some other man's son. Still, I couldn't blame Mom. We'd always been alike in that way, needing to be held and cared for. No, I'd say Zach Sr. had it coming. And, anyway, who was he to complain? Loyalty had never mattered to him, at least not him being loyal.

My younger brother Leo had his own ways to make ends meet, and at the ripe age of 10, he became a drug dealer, walking the streets at night when he should have been sleeping in bed or doing his homework. I started sleeping at friends' houses just to avoid going home after Mom took up with Marvin. He filled in the empty place Dad once occupied, but I couldn't stand to see his face with his knowing grin. I couldn't stand the feeling that he was a giant leech, sucking the life out of our home. I imagined he only stayed for the free room and board, skimpy as it was.

If Dad was bad, Marvin was a nightmare. In his way, he loved my mom. At least he was gentle with his hands, he stuck around and didn't go after other women. Still, it was like he couldn't hold her close enough, and Leo and I were just something to take Mom's attention from him. He moved in and officially became my stepdad, and I began to dream of getting out. Of going someplace where sirens weren't always wailing into the starless skies. Where Marvin wasn't waiting to compete for my mom's attention and where I could be my own man, out from under the collapsing roof of my life. Music became my escape. I made my own sounds, my own rhymes and beats, to quiet the demons. I knew if I could just rap, if I could just make it big, I could be like those guys with all the money and ladies and respect. I could buy Mom a house and take her out of there, and she'd be proud and wouldn't need to work or drink away her fears and sorrows because she'd be so happy. If only I could just break in to the music industry, all of my problems would be over.

But breaking in wasn't as easy as I thought it would be, no matter how many people told me I had talent, that I was going places. I just kept on living my life, like I was running but going no place.

Late one night, Mom shook me, and I felt I was being pulled out of a long black tunnel.

"Zach. Zach." My mom's harsh whisper broke into the fog.

"What is it, Mama?"

"It's Leo. Your brother's been shot."

I jumped out of bed, stumbling, pulling my thin too-large jeans on, and grabbing my jacket. "Let's go. I'm ready."

Rushing to the hospital that night was like heading toward a train wreck. The city blurred past, all part of the nightmare. The streets weren't empty, though they should have been if it were any kind of place to live. No, people stood, shirtless men with hands jammed in pockets trying to look like they weren't up to no good, women wearing skimpy tops and tight pants, newspaper pages rolling like tumbleweeds down the sidewalk, homeless folks curled up like snails on bus stop benches or dark shop entrances, and groups of fools huddling like vultures waiting to swoop in on the next unsuspecting person. No, this was no place to live. Only a place to die. We pulled in to the emergency room side of the hospital, the fluorescent lights making my mom's face look more drawn and gray-pale.

"My son, he checked himself in earlier. Had a gunshot wound." She said it in a whisper as if ashamed to be heard, even though most of the folks there wouldn't have cared since they were strung out or had seen too much suffering of their own to bother with us.

The nurse looked down at a clipboard, then tapped on the keys of her computer as if she were checking out a book, not whether my brother was dead or alive. She looked up at us, wary, squinting her eyes. "He's in surgery right now." She shook her head, accusation in her eyes. "How old is your boy, ma'am?"

Mom put her hands on the tall counter, dropping her head down so it almost touched the dull surface, then said more softly, as if it took all the energy she had to utter the word, "Twelve."

Silence. Shame hovered like a cloud. A line of black crows on an endless dilapidated fence, stretching as far as the eye could see.

"Thanks." I guided Mom to the waiting room chairs, and together we sat down without saying a word. Waiting for news. Wondering how the world had gotten so dark and ugly.

My brother survived and told us later that he had been shot while out driving with a friend. *Driving and dealing,* I thought. He managed to get himself to the hospital without wrecking the car. Mom got worse after that. She struggled to make enough to pay rent and put food on the table, and she couldn't seem to bear the fact that one of her boys would most likely not make it into his teens. Somehow she managed to get cheap liquor, needing it like medicine to blur the sharp edges of her life, help her find peace, pretend she was happy. Many nights I sat up late helping her through a drinking binge, her shaky hands lifting cigarette after cigarette to her dry lips, taking sips of strong black coffee. It was like watching something deteriorate right in front of me but having no way to stop it, to put the pieces back together. An ache grew so deep in my chest at times I felt I might bust apart into a million tiny pieces, shards of glass flung across a dingy floor.

I had to get out. Everything was falling apart. I couldn't stick around and end up like my brother. Like my mom. At 16, I got a job at an optical shop and was soon the top salesperson. As soon as I could, I moved out and got my own place and pursued my music, taking gigs rapping whenever they opened up, though few paid anything. I felt hope for the first time in a long time and imagined myself finally making a name for myself, and then I could laugh at my past and it would just be a good story of rags to riches.

Somehow — I still can't even figure out how it happened — I got married to a woman who was only interested in a thrill. Not long after the wedding, I found out Sylvia was sleeping with someone else, and since I didn't need that, didn't want to be some pitiful throw-away, I told her to leave. I had bought the house, after all, and she hadn't done anything but mooch since day one. Still, one day at work I got a call from my neighbor Ben.

"Dude, Sylvia's at the house."

"What? Why?"

"Don't know. But she's hauling a bunch of stuff out to a truck with some guy."

I had no car, and the woman knew it would take me hours to get home because I had to take several buses. She had planned it that way. Users know how to take advantage like that.

"Thanks, man."

"What should I do?" He sounded angry, like he was ready to fight for my things.

"Nothing. It's not worth it."

When I got home that night the place was stripped bare, including the shower knobs. The only thing left was a mattress in the center of my bedroom. I flicked the switch, cutting the light. It was better not to sit there thinking of everything she had taken from me, especially because it had been more than what my house could hold. Better to just be in the dark. So I did. Maybe I should have been sad and cried or yelled or something, but I was more relieved than anything. She was gone, and since she'd taken everything, she wouldn't be back. No reason to. I lay down on the mattress and went to sleep.

I threw myself into my work, and it felt good to be making money after watching my mom scrape by like she had. It gave me a sense of control and peace of mind. We talked on the phone, Mom and I. Talked about everything. She always listened well, offering "Mmm-hmms" in all the right places. Never judging me for anything I said or did, even the marriage, since she had seen her fair share of grief. She'd been used, too.

I worked so much and it took me so long to get home on the buses that I rarely went out. Still, Ben convinced me to go with him and his cousin to a new club downtown one Saturday night. I dressed up and decided since I'd most likely not go again for a while, I might as well go all out, even spraying on some cologne and checking myself in the mirror more than once before heading out the door.

When we arrived, the music throbbed, and strobe lights pulsed. People packed the place, and electricity seemed to pulse in my chest. I took a slow drink of my Bacardi and Coke and willed myself to relax, feeling the beat in my chest, itching to dance. Yeah, it had definitely been too long since I'd just had some fun.

"Dude, see that girl over there?" I didn't, but I went along with it. "She's hot." Ben looked like a dog scoping out a bone.

Since it seemed pointless to try to yell over the din, I just nodded.

He took that as encouragement because before I knew it, he snaked his way in that direction. I followed and stood slightly behind my friend as he leaned in to the girl and asked her to dance. Seconds later, he led her to the dance floor, leaving me standing there with the girl's friend. Just like that, I felt like a teenager trying to find my game. I took her in for the first time. Petite, Hispanic, dark silky hair, mysterious. She stood there holding her drink, totally relaxed, like it didn't make her uncomfortable not to talk. Like she had no place to go but was okay with that. She looked out at the dance floor, then flicked her eyes at me, then back out again.

"What's your name?" I yelled.

She shook her head and leaned in. "What?"

"Your name."

"I'm Sonya." She said it close to my ear so I could hear her voice over the noise, the warmth of her breath giving me goose bumps.

"I'm Zach." I spoke against her hair, resisting the urge to rub it between my fingers. I caught the scent of her perfume, sweet and musky.

"Dance?" I moved a little to give her the gist.

She nodded and smiled, revealing dimples. She was adorable.

I led the way, holding her small hand in mine, guiding her through the throng of people. And just like that the music changed, and a salsa beat replaced the hip-hop one from seconds before. I shook my head to show her I had no idea what to do. She just grinned and began moving in a sexy way, her Latin roots shining through, and I had no other option but to fake it. I watched the guy beside me, trying to mimic his moves, laughing a little at how funny I must look but not caring, either. Sonya put her hands on my arms, a butterfly touch with only her fingertips, but it still felt warm, and I wished she wouldn't take them away. But then the song ended, and we moved off the dance floor, finding a back table, away from all the noise.

"Want to know what I was doing just an hour before I got here?" She leaned toward me and offered a sly smile.

"What were you doing?"

"Guess."

"Hmm." I played along. "Milking a cow?"

"No."

"Chopping wood?"

"No. Nothing that funny."

I offered a skeptical raise of an eyebrow.

She laughed, and the sound made me smile back.

"I was in my PJs, my hair in a bun, watching a movie. My friend had to practically drag me out of the house."

"Really?" I tried to imagine her that way, then shook my head since I knew that picture wouldn't be helpful in making me appear gentlemanly. "Yeah, Ben told me I would miss out on the best night of my life if I stayed home. Called me an old man. I couldn't let him be right."

Sonya put her elbows on the table and propped her chin on her hands. "I'm glad I came out."

"Me, too."

We danced all the rest of the night together, sneaking off in between to talk and get drinks. The last song was slow. Holding her, it seemed like we were the only two people in the place, even though we were pressed on all sides by a sweaty crowd. The rhythm swayed around us, and I leaned in, kissing her softly, tasting the wine she had just finished, wrapping my arms around her back, loving how small she felt in my hands, against my chest.

She spoke into my neck, "I need you to know something before you get too carried away here."

She pulled back slightly so I could see her dark eyes in the dim room, the shape of her mouth. "I have two kids." Somehow the confession didn't surprise or bother me. "They're 1 and 3." She waited.

"Okay."

"Does that bother you?" Her eyebrows were two dark arches against her creamy skin.

"No, why should it?"

"Well, because it usually does bother most guys."

"Hmm. Not me."

She seemed to appraise me, squinting her eyes slightly, then allowed her head to rest against my shoulder. "Okay. Just wanted you to know."

"Thanks for telling me." And I meant it. Something about her willingness to be honest and vulnerable told me I could trust her. She was nothing like Sylvia. Nothing like any of the people who had slithered their way into my mom's heart throughout the years. And she had a quiet strength that made me relax. Made me feel safe but on fire at the same time.

Outside, we talked, holding hands facing each other. "Can I have your number?"

"Well, I don't usually hand out my number to just anyone." She smiled up at me.

"Well, how about I give you mine first?"

"Okay." She held up her cell, and I added my number to her contacts.

"Now, your turn." I pulled out my phone and watched her under the streetlight as she typed in her information, somewhat relieved that the dimly lit club hadn't misled me but also thinking her looks were only slightly important. We had connected in a way I had never experienced with another woman before.

Had it been the liquor? Had I imagined the spark or was she feeling it, too?

"I'll call you."

"Please do." With that she let go of my hand and walked with her friends to their car.

Ben crowded in and draped his arm over my shoulders. "Find true love?" I would definitely be the one driving us home.

And as crazy as it seemed, I wondered if I *had* and hoped that the next day it wouldn't turn out to be just another night out. But somehow I doubted that.

I waited three days before clicking on Sonya's contact and pressing the call button.

"Hi." Her voice sounded nice without the blasting music competing for attention.

"Hi."

Quiet. "I was hoping you'd call."

"You were?"

"Yep." Her laugh sounded soft and comfortable.

"Can I take you out?"

"Yes, you can." I loved the easygoing way she had about her. The way she didn't pretend to be aloof or afraid to show her interest.

"I don't have a car." The confession embarrassed me, but I figured she might as well know. Showing up on my bicycle might be funny but somewhat unimpressive.

"I do. I can pick you up if that doesn't offend your masculinity."

"Well, maybe it does a little, but under the circumstances it sounds like the best plan."

We talked for a long time after that, setting the date and time and reluctantly hanging up. All week my thoughts were on Sonya and going places in my mind that were foolish and adolescent, but I didn't care. It seemed like she was the girl I had been waiting for without even realizing it.

I took her out to a nice Italian place, loving the way the candlelight flickered on her skin, mesmerized by the sweet grin she offered and the way she tucked her hair behind her small ear. After that, we were inseparable. Aside from the time I was working, we spent most every evening together. I even enjoyed time with her kids, thinking that even though every example of fatherhood in my life had been a joke, I could be different. Better. I determined to surprise even myself.

After Sylvia left, I'd had to get roommates, but they turned out to be deadbeats and weren't paying rent, so there I was, stuck with a mortgage I could no longer afford and feeling like it wasn't worth it since I spent so much time at Sonya's place, anyway. So I gave it up and moved in with her, feeling somehow that I was home for the very first time. It wasn't quite what we had planned, but six months later, I was still there, and Sonya was pregnant. We were in love, and life felt good.

Deep down, I still longed to pursue my music, convinced that if I could only just make it in that business, I wouldn't have to bust my butt at the optical place and would finally have enough money to buy a car and actually go places and do all the things I always dreamed of. So I went after that dream again, trying to force my foot in the door to the rap world, little by little. Rhythms and words beat out in my head. And I wanted to get them out into the world so badly.

Sonya was pregnant and ready to pop.

She stood in the bedroom, looking in the tall mirror, wearing overalls and a striped shirt, looking beautiful and round.

"I feel fat." She frowned at her figure, eyebrows low and her mouth pouting. I covered a smile.

Moving behind her and wrapping my arms around her belly, I nuzzled into her neck and said, "No. You look beautiful."

"No, I don't. I'm enormous."

"You have a whole other human being in your body."

"Yeah, but …"

"And when I look at you, I only see someone I love." I rubbed my hands all over her belly, like it was a crystal ball.

We were getting ready for the co-ed baby shower our friends had planned for us. Sonya pulled her hair up in a ponytail and turned to face me, having to move back a foot to accommodate for the baby between us.

"Promise?"

"Promise."

I asked my girl to marry me that day in front of all our friends, but first I had taken Sonya's parents out and asked for their blessing. Thankfully, they gave it. I knew I wanted to be a part of a family like hers — one with a dad and a mom and one who spent time together and shared each other's problems and joys. They weren't perfect, but they seemed to love each other, and I had never had that kind of family myself, and I longed for that maybe as much as I longed to marry Sonya. So there she sat at the baby shower, gift wrap littered around her tennis shoes, looking completely uncomfortable and awkward and round when I popped the question. She seemed so surprised, like she couldn't believe I would possibly want such a thing in her current condition. But she smiled, her brown eyes wide and small creases forming in the corners, looking so happy.

"Yes!" Deep contentment registered in her eyes.

We got married and were so happy and so alive. The day my baby boy was born was like the world exploding, then reforming into something better and new, with new roads and pathways where I'd only seen dead-end streets before. My wife giving birth filled me with such a deep sense of awe at this woman who had sacrificed so much for us to be a family and at the new life that filled me with purpose like never before. I couldn't help but cry, my body and mind were so full of emotion. I cut the thick cord that connected our baby's body to Sonya's and swallowed the burn in my throat.

Being a dad and husband made me feel even more determined to find a way to break into music. I needed to take care of them and find a way to ensure our lives wouldn't be like my childhood had been. When I rapped, I felt the doubts and insecurities and the sense that my world was a fragile place all melt away. I felt empowered by the words, like I was chanting strength against the weakness, I was speaking anger and rebellion over poverty, I was screaming at that weak little boy and telling him to get up and make something of himself and quit scratching out a living like a beggar. The words swirled through me, pumped my body with pride, and I knew this was what I needed to do with my life. Nothing else. I couldn't settle for anything less. Still, it wasn't easy. It pulled me away from Sonya and the kids, and that took its toll on both of us. But she supported me and wanted me to chase after that dream, knowing it was the only thing that would get us out of the "just making it" cycle.

I was gone more regularly on the weekends, doing gigs and taking whatever offers came my way. I had formed a group, and we were making a name for ourselves. We all believed that if we just put in the time, it could be easy street down the road. We'd have everything we needed. We'd have money and respect and would never have to wonder about a meal or never have to deny ourselves anything. I cut back on my hours at the optical place, knowing that was getting in my way of being able to MC, knowing sacrifices were necessary to success. And eventually I quit there altogether so I could accept an offer anytime it came my way. But it seemed like I was spinning my wheels, running in place, and some days all I wanted was to quit. When I was home, I just wanted to relax since it felt like all I ever did was try and try and try. I longed for down time, for a safe place to quit working so hard every second of the day, a safe place to not have it all together and say all the right things.

Sonya took the brunt of the housework and also worked full time, but we had both agreed to the arrangement so her growing edge whenever I was home irked me.

"Zach, this isn't working. You need to go back to work. We barely have enough money for groceries." She stuffed my socks into the laundry basket, glaring at me like I'd just committed a crime.

I grunted as I adjusted my place on the couch, hooking my gaze on the video game flashing on the screen. "Baby, I know it's hard, but I've got a show this weekend, and I just know it's going to pan out."

"You keep saying that. How long have you been saying that, Zach? We're going deeper and deeper in the hole."

She was right about that. Recording and producing the album and traveling had cost money. Being new to the scene, our band was rarely paid well, if at all. But we had agreed to this. We both knew we couldn't just give up after spending so much and working so hard.

"Trust me, we're almost there. And then you won't have to do anything. Hey, we can even get a maid to do the laundry." I nodded toward the basket she was holding like a shield, then flashed a grin, hoping she'd move on and quit nagging.

She turned and left the room, sighing loud enough for me to hear, and I bit my tongue, knowing it would only worsen her mood to tell her to knock it off.

But things just deteriorated between us. I took every gig I could get, meaning I was home less and less. But still I chased the dream because up on stage, it seemed, was the only place I got any respect. The crowd cheered so loud sometimes my ears buzzed and I felt so alive — I knew that music was my lifeblood.

People yelled out or danced along to the music, and the connection was almost tangible. Real. Nothing else filled me anymore the way two hours on the stage could. Coming home felt dreary and stagnant in comparison. How could I possibly get a mundane job after that? Any day the money would come. Any day I'd be discovered and not just as a part of someone else's fame. No, it would be me they'd be asking for. I'd be famous.

But that day didn't come. It was one rabbit trail after another, chasing the dangling carrot.

"What now, Zach?" The high-pitched way she said my name made me cringe. Nothing like the way she said it the night we met. I wished I could change things back to the time when she believed in my dreams. In our future. But the world had become a place of mere survival somehow, without color or hope, and I felt it might snuff the life out of me. "What about me? What about the kids?"

"I don't care about you and the kids!" I screamed, adding an expletive. The words left my mouth before I even had time to think them through, like they'd been waiting to be said, like I had stored them up to use when I needed to hurt my wife so she'd know I wasn't one to be talked down to day in and day out. I screamed the words and instantly felt sick to my stomach. I was nothing but a loser, like my so-called dad. And now I was using words to slap Sonya in the face with all of my pent-up frustration. It wasn't her fault things hadn't worked out. I stood up and reached for her, but she flinched and her eyes shone with tears. "I didn't mean that." Somehow *those* words barely came out. She just turned and left the house. I heard the sound of the car starting and pulling out and then just quiet. Just me and an empty house and the terrible realization that I hadn't amounted to anything, despite all my plans.

The chasm between Sonya and me only grew after that. She quit trying to get me to be home more to spend time with her and the kids. It was like she made a decision to stop. She was a stone-cold statue whenever I was around. When I reached for her in bed, she tensed and rolled over, and the dark silhouette of her body felt miles away. I tried not to allow any of my skin to touch hers, certain it repulsed her. I wouldn't force myself on her. She'd have to make the first move because I couldn't stand the rejection of her recoiling or hugging me like a wooden doll, or seeing the blank way she looked at me as if I weren't even there and she was looking at something else, living someplace else in her mind.

We agreed that it was time to just get a divorce.

"Don't you love me anymore?" I ventured into the quiet of the kitchen. Somehow the small space echoed with my hurt.

She looked through me. "I do love you." Then she turned away, all her attention focused on cutting a carrot. "I'm just not in love with you anymore."

The ache in my chest was so strong, I felt I might fall apart right there, pieces of a man, powerless and broken.

I moved out of the house and in with a buddy of mine, hoping it would be for just a little while. I'd make it in music and then she'd want me back. Then she'd want to touch me. I came home only to visit with the kids or pick them up for the weekend. I hoped my absence would make Sonya miss me. That it would make her realize what she'd pushed away. But one afternoon I came to the house and only my 12-year-old daughter was home. The house was quiet and seemed abandoned.

"Where's your mom?" I had the divorce papers back at the apartment on the kitchen table under a box of cereal. I couldn't bring myself to sign them. I loved Sonya, but I couldn't make her love me back. I wanted her to look at me and see something different, someone who had done something with his life. I wanted her to be proud.

My daughter Maggie shrugged. "At a friend's house." I could tell she wasn't telling the whole story.

"Is this friend a man?"

She nodded, and something inside me ripped right down the middle. "Has he been staying overnight here?"

She shook her head slowly, then said, "No, we've been staying over there."

Maggie wouldn't look at me. Wouldn't respond, just sat still as a stone, except for the small movement of her hand squeezing a nubby pencil. Everything seemed to snap all at once. Like a house made of twigs up against a gale-force wind. My throat felt hot and thick, and I thought I might puke, but somehow I managed to hold myself together. At least until I was alone. And then I cried like a baby in the darkness of my friend's apartment, knowing that anything that ever mattered was no longer mine. I was my mom, and I was alone.

But I refused to be the victim. It was time to get things right. To get myself right. A while before, I had met Pastor Jeff from New Hope International Church, and he had invited me to visit. Sonya and I had gone a few times, but it had never been anything more than just visiting, like we were going to a play or something. It didn't sink in, I knew that. But I felt that going might help me figure out the mess of my life. Might help me turn things back to something good, at least in my own heart.

So I stepped into the church that night, and it felt like God himself ushered me in, guided me down the aisle to my seat. Everything about that moment felt supernatural — an out-of-body experience almost. The pastor started preaching, and it was as if every word he said was for me. I knew I had become a self-centered poser, but somehow, in that place, even surrounded by hundreds of other people, I felt singled out by Jesus. Like he was sitting there with me, pressing his forehead to mine, reminding me that my success wasn't based on flimsy man-made ideals of fame and fortune. No, my value came from the maker of heaven and earth creating me, loving me and laying down his life for me. Thinking about how Jesus Christ walked this earth, I saw how different it was from my own strivings. He hadn't tried to make himself great. He simply *was.* He led others as a servant might, washing the crusty feet of "nobodies," hanging out with whores and losers. But me? I had sold my soul to the crowds. To my own personal god of fame. And it had left me feeling like a slug, with no backbone, no value.

Spending time with God felt like all those nights of stroking my mom's hair and talking her through her drunkenness, holding her and expecting nothing in return except her love. That's what it was like, only I was the fool fighting my own demons, and God was quieting me and reminding me that no matter what, I was loved. The sensation broke me and, somehow, at the very same time, rebuilt me, too.

"Who am I, God?" I whispered. Not knowing what he wanted. Not knowing what to do next.

You are mine.

Things started to change for me that day at the church, a slow, steady healing and deepening of my faith in Jesus. A slow, steady release of my own plans and dreams to him. And, also, things with Sonya seemed to be changing. I told her I was sorry for the man I had failed to be, the dad I'd failed to be. And though skepticism marked her features at first, I began to see something different when I'd come by the house for the kids. Her look changed. She told me she had ended things with the other man and wanted to try again. She told me she was sorry, and since I knew she had seen that same pattern with people close to her, of infidelity, of escaping to someone else's arms when things got hard, I understood. I had seen it in my own home, too. We were both broken people when we began playing house for ourselves.

So we started attending church together, as a family, and my wife transformed before me. From a tightly wrapped cocoon to a butterfly. From a plastic cut-out to a flesh and blood woman. Back from the dead. She began to reach for my hand again, stroking a thumb over the top of mine, leaning in to me and allowing me to draw her close. Something had chipped away at her shell, and I saw the woman I'd met years before, soft and vulnerable and beautiful.

"It's not too late, is it?" Sonya leaned her head on my shoulder. We sat together on the couch in the living room, the *tick, tick, tick* of the clock reminding me to enjoy the moment.

I turned to face her and saw tears brimming in her eyes. "For what?"

"We don't have to go through with the divorce, do we?" She leaned closer in, searching me for the answer.

Stroking her cheek with my thumb, I answered, "We'll figure out how to call it off."

"Okay." She sighed deep and slow, as though releasing the entire weight of the world.

And things were good for a while.

But when I couldn't seem to get enough work, I began dreaming of my music again, trying to imagine it finally reaching the public. Then Sonya and I could quit worrying constantly, every minute of every day, about the mountain of debt I'd created for us. I felt defeated every time I thought about all the things we needed but couldn't buy. I couldn't even afford to buy my wife clothes to replace the threadbare ones she wore. I felt like a real man should be able to do at least that. At the very least.

I still thought music could bring in enough money to make our struggles all go away. And so I began to try again. I worked to get gigs, but nothing brought me the riches that I saw others achieve. I looked at the other MCs I knew and wondered if they couldn't buy their wives clothes they needed. Pathetic. That's what I felt like.

Still I spun my wheels, did my thing, tried to reach that dream. When we were asked to join a headliner on tour, it seemed the break had finally come. Then Sonya would see she had worried for nothing, and she'd apologize for not being more supportive and would respect me for having not given up when things got hard. I fortified myself with that and allowed my pride to swell back up again. Finally. Finally I would get what I wanted. What I'd always wanted.

But like all fragile things do, it fell apart like it had no more stability than sand in the wind. One member of our group was getting married and decided he didn't want to do the music scene anymore. And just like that, the whole thing fell apart. Without the whole group, the deal was off. I couldn't bear to think about the way Sonya would look at me when I told her that I'd failed again. I knew the look well. I kneeled down in the center of my kitchen and called out to God in the middle of that space and said, "I'm begging you to make me famous! That's all I'm asking of you! I just want to make music." The words seemed to bounce around like ping-pong balls in an empty container, not going up and out into the sky but just ricocheting in the silence, making me feel more lost and alone than ever.

Though I had the hope of Christ, I allowed the old lies to soak in like acid. *You're not a man. You've gotten nowhere in your life. You'll end up just like your mom, striving all the time but never making it.*

The old feeling of separation between Sonya and me returned, inch by inch.

I knew I was doing it again, creating the gaping canyon, but it was like my programming kept turning me to the wrong thing. Over and over and over. Then one sweltering afternoon, I got the call from my mom.

"Son?"

"Hi, Mom." *Did I imagine she sounded different? Like the fire in her had been put out?*

"Son, I need you to come to the hospital. But I don't want you making a fuss. Everything is going to be just fine." She soothed me before she even said what was wrong.

"What's going to be just fine?"

"I am."

"Why? What's wrong?"

"We'll talk about it when you get here, all right?" No, not all right. Nothing was all right.

"I'll be there." The urgency to see her, to touch her face, to press back the darkness for her overwhelmed me, and I dressed quickly, forgetting to grab anything to eat on the way out the door.

The drive to the hospital felt endless, cars packed in, like a funeral procession.

After getting directions to her room, I sprinted down the antiseptic halls of the hospital ward.

I rounded the corner and found the room number, then knocked and entered before waiting for her to tell me to come in. And when I saw her, I knew. She was dying, with one foot in the grave already. A sob caught in my throat, and I swallowed the pain, willing myself to have the words, to offer hope and laughter. But I couldn't do it.

"Mama?" I realized I'd said it like I didn't believe it was her.

"Zach." She said my name so exhausted, like she had no fight left in her.

"Why didn't you tell me?"

"Didn't want you to worry."

"You said it was going to be all right." I ground out the words, forcing them past my panic, past the tears and into the room, a challenge to a stubborn woman who never backed down from a fight.

"I know I did, and it will."

"But it won't be. Look at you. You're …" I held in the rest knowing it wouldn't do any good. This was a losing battle. "Oh, Mama." I gingerly rested my head on her stomach and cried, wishing for the first time since I was little that I could go back and spend more time with her, even if it meant she was working off a hangover. I sobbed into the blankets, feeling her hand on the back of my neck.

"Shh."

Knowing my mom had so little time nearly killed me. One night after work, I went to see her, and she didn't even know who I was. The cancer seemed to be eating her alive, and every time I went, more of her was gone. Each time I left the hospital, the pain felt so strong and so real it might as well have been a lion tearing me to pieces, bit by bit. The headlights of the oncoming traffic were like a million eyes, watching me, waiting for me to fall apart. And I didn't care anymore.

The money problems, the distance between Sonya and me, my mom dying in the hospital and the realization that no matter how hard I tried, I would never succeed. It all just seemed to swallow me up. I pressed on the gas thinking about how I could just end it. Then Sonya and the kids would have the insurance money from my death, and I wouldn't have to watch my mom waste away, and I could just go be at peace with Jesus, singing in the heavenly choir. I gripped the steering wheel thinking that the easiest thing would be to turn into the oncoming traffic and then fly off the craggy hillside and disappear. It wouldn't hurt because who could survive a fall like that? And then it would be over with. I turned the wheel slightly, veering off to the left, but at the same time I felt something pulling the steering wheel back the other way, counterbalancing my efforts.

God, why?! Tears blurred my vision, but the sensation that it wasn't meant to end this way, the feeling that this was the wrong way out, counseled me back to the center of the lane. I allowed my leg to relax, back off the gas pedal and just drive the long road home, the gray-black night blurring past me. My numbness nearly consumed me, like I was in a walking coma. Voices and words sounded muted and didn't get through my fog. The day my stepdad called to say that Mom had passed away just blended in with the darkness of my world. In my heart, I had already lost her, already pulled back from the pain, like a child drawing away from fire. So his call only deepened the pain a little.

Pastor Jeff and his wife, Missy, reached out and then just kept pursuing Sonya and me. Little by little, I felt myself pulling out of the darkness, remembering where my value came from. Remembering to love my wife and kids and quit being so self-centered. Slowly I began to crawl out of my pit and blink into the light of day.

I made a decision to give up pursing a career in music. It was the thing I couldn't seem to balance, and I needed time to fall in love with Jesus, to romance my wife and grow down my roots, deep and healthy and strong.

And when I did that, when I gave up that idol, I felt something in me fall into place. I needed to release my tight grip and hold everything in my life with hands wide open. It's funny how releasing can tend to bring the one thing you wanted back, but in a healthy kind of way. Like birds flying off into the sky but coming home to land now and then on that healthy tree branch.

Somehow, opportunities came along to tour and rap. Sonya and I agreed that it could work, but only if it didn't control me anymore. I couldn't work for music like a slave to his master. It could be part of my life, but not the controlling part anymore.

Pursuing music in a more healthy fashion, I found other joys, not the least of which was time and intimacy with Sonya. She became my best song. She was the gift I needed all along, and I felt sure that she was given to me by the very hand of God. Together we started basking in the limelight of Christ, the rhythm of our lives woven into a bigger plan, a bigger song. And nothing sounded better than that.

FULL SPEED AHEAD
The Story of Bernie
Written by Alexine Garcia

He wanted 14 ounces of meth and 7 ounces of coke. I had bad vibes about the whole thing, so I packed less merchandise. Even with the strange vibes, I couldn't turn down a sale. My gut warned me to play it safe this time. I usually never left the house without packing my two guns — a Beretta tucked in my front waistband and a 22 down the back of my pants. But this time I left them behind. I got in the car and drove to meet him at Montgomery Ward's.

"Go ahead and park where you always park," I heard him say on the phone. My stomach turned. I just had a bad feeling about the whole thing. I parked my car, and before I knew it, the muzzle of a gun was right in my face. "FREEZE!" a cop shouted. "Put your hands on the steering wheel or I'll blow your head off."

৵৵৵

I lay in bed smiling up at my wall of accolades. It had been a good year for me. You better believe I was the best at everything I did. My mom hung the proof above my bed — every medal, award and even my report cards. I started wrestling at the YMCA, and I was good at it, too. I had the highest grades in most of my classes, especially biology, which earned me a spot in a gifted science program with NYU Medical Center. I got to help with animal research. Then I auditioned for a repertory theater production with Meri Mini Players. Five thousand kids tried out, and only five of us made it. Everything was going my way, and I was only 12 years old. I was the best baseball player in my neighborhood, too. On top of it all, I was a pretty good-looking guy. I actually modeled for three years.

I always say I couldn't have come from better soil. My dad was a hard worker, gone from 8 a.m. to 5 p.m. every day. He came home to my mom who kept an immaculate household. Growing up in a Puerto Rican family in Manhattan with two of the best parents was not too shabby. I had some fine role models to encourage me in all my goals.

When I started high school, it only got better. I imagined my future like the bright ballpark lights of Yankee Stadium illuminating the whole field. You can see those lights miles away, and I sure could see a bright future in the distance for me. I was the captain of the wrestling and baseball teams by my junior year. Upon graduation, I had my pick of athletic and academic scholarships. That science program when I was 12 sparked my interest in animals. So, I chose an athletic scholarship with Farmingdale State College on Long Island so that I could major in veterinary medicine. From what I could see, my life was about to get really good, but my mom had different plans for me.

"Bernie, Long Island is too far away. There are plenty of good schools to choose from right here in New York. We got NYU, St. John's and Columbia. You could take your pick."

"Mom, biology is my best subject. I can't study what I want at those schools." I couldn't believe that she wanted to stand in the way of my dream.

"Helena, he has a scholarship. Let the boy go, he'll be fine," Dad chimed in.

But she wasn't having it. She stood at the stove stirring a pot of one of her delicious meals. Her whole body moved with her whisking arm. She shot a scowl over to my dad, which silenced anything else he was going to say.

"Mom, please," I begged with tears running down my face. She just couldn't accept the thought of me anywhere else except right in her home.

John Jay College of Criminal Justice had an excellent baseball team, so I settled for that. I let the thought of it comfort the loss of going to my dream school and becoming a veterinarian.

Confusion buzzed within every inch of my mind as one dream after another faded. I saw those bright stadium lights in my future shutting down, one by one.

Criminal justice was my new major, becoming a lawyer was my new goal, but it made me feel empty inside. I was confused.

I needed a way to pay for college after enrolling in a school that hadn't offered me scholarships, so I took the New York Police Department entrance exam.

"Look, Bernie," Jacob said to me, shaking his letter in my face. "I aced my test, man!"

"That's great! I'm still looking out for my letter."

He raced up the stairs of the stoop I was sitting on to go show his parents the good news. I walked up the stairs and into our apartment. Mom was mopping the floor. The veins in her arms bulged as she put her back into her work.

"Mama, where's the mailbox key?"

"Como que mailbox key?" she asked spiritedly. "This is my house. I check the mail here."

"Well, go check the mail then. I'm waiting for my test scores from the police department."

"Can't you see I'm working? I will check the mail when I have time."

I walked down the hall to my room, lay down and stared up at my wall of accolades. Perhaps things were going to look up after all. I just wanted some clear-cut direction in my life.

The next day, I was walking home with my books tucked under my arm when Fred ran up next to me. "Hey, Bernie! Did you get your scores yet?" He clutched a letter in his hands.

"No, not yet. Still waiting."

"Well, if anyone got in, it's you, man. We'll be training together before long. You'll see."

I sure hope he's right. This was getting old.

I was walking up the stairs to my apartment, and the disappointment was just too much. I trudged across the fourth-floor hall to our apartment as tears flowed down my face. Months had passed since I took that exam, and I was sure I aced it. My middle brother, Bobby, was walking down the hall toward me, and I knew he could see my tears.

"Why you crying? What's going on?"

I just looked at him and leaned up against the wall. He started to cry, too.

"Bernie, man. I got to tell you something. Don't look for that letter no more."

I stood up from the wall and looked him in the face. "What do you mean?"

"Your letter came a long time ago. Mom threw it down the incinerator. She don't want you to be a cop. She just doesn't want to see you get killed." His body shook as he held his head and cried. I was crying, too. I was furious, snot and tears running down my face.

I sat at the dinner table and opened my schoolbooks. Homework was nothing new to me, but this, this criminal justice crap was boring. Becoming a lawyer was my goal, but it wasn't my passion. It was just something to get by.

I read the same paragraph over and over. It just wouldn't stick with the anger rolling in my head. My mom walked through the front door a few hours later with bags of groceries.

"Is it true, Mama? Did you throw away my police letter?"

She stopped in the doorway holding plastic bags of groceries for a moment, looking for the words to say.

"*Mijo*, it's such a dangerous job. I don't want you to get killed."

"Ma! This is craziness! How could you do this to me?"

"There are so many other jobs out there. You'll find something good, son."

I walked down the hall and slammed the door to my room. I was heading nowhere fast. Baseball was gone. Veterinarian school was gone. Becoming a police officer was gone. What was I supposed to do? I was an award winner. I was a team captain. I was an A student. But you wouldn't know it by looking at me anymore.

I went about my life in a haze. As a family, we went to a Catholic church every Sunday. I prayed as I sat on the long wooden pew, but deep down I just felt empty and worthless.

A few weeks later, I was ironing my uniform for my first day of work. It wasn't a cop uniform or baseball duds, but being a security guard would have to do. I combed my hair, looking at my refection in the mirror. I didn't like what I saw. I just didn't know who I was anymore. My roots ran deep in that good soil, so I went to work and worked hard one day after the next just like my dad. I received one promotion after another and ended up as a lieutenant.

Drinking and partying just wasn't my thing, so an assignment working as a bouncer at a club was a whole new experience. The dark room illuminated by flashing lights, skimpily dressed women, blaring music — it was a lot to take in.

I walked around the dance floor making my way to the bathroom on my 10-minute break. The light was bright in there, and nobody was hiding his deeds. Men led gorgeous girls in and found an empty stall and proceeded to grope and kiss right there in the bathroom.

Those are some pretty ladies with those ugly dudes. What's wrong with me that girls like that don't look my way? I could hear the long inhaling snorts of cocaine from behind closed stall doors.

"Hey. What's your name?" a man smoking asked me, looking me up and down.

"Bernie."

"You oughta try this." He nodded to his friend cutting a line of coke on the bathroom counter.

"Thanks all the same. That's not my thing." I nodded and walked out of the bathroom. It was a shock to see all this debauchery happening in front of me. It was even more shocking watching these people act like it was commonplace.

The second time I encountered him in the bathroom was just like the first. "This is the good stuff," he said with a smirk.

"No, that's not my thing. Thanks, anyway."

This guy was persistent because a week later he was right there in that same bathroom, with his same shiny suit and polyester button-up shirt asking me that same question.

"Coke just ain't for me."

Two weeks later, my resolve began to weaken.

"Listen, how can you really knock something you have never tried? You're not gonna get high or go nuts. This ain't like other drugs. This is going to help you stay up and be alert on the job. Have a drink, and you won't even feel it."

What did I have to lose? Maybe he was right. Besides all that, I figured, I had nothing else good going for me. How was I supposed to know this wasn't my thing if I hadn't even tried it? His friend cut me a line, and it stung as I inhaled it through a straw. But he was right. Once I got passed the initial burn, I felt wide awake and ready for anything. The phrase "high as a kite" made so much sense right then. I was up, up, up.

I met him in the bathroom from time to time, maybe once a month, and we split lines together. Then I got used to the idea, and it became once a week. I started changing in the bathroom and joining the crowd on the dance floor after work. I never really was a drinker before, but I could start to see why all these people were having so much fun. And believe me, I could dance. I impressed all those pretty girls with my salsa and merengue moves.

೪೪೪

My parents were straight-laced, I guess you could say. My mother had never even seen cocaine, or any drug for that matter, until she found it in my room. My dad really couldn't believe I was on drugs. Deep down, he really wanted to believe my lies. My father feared I was possessed. He took me to a Catholic church, but not the one we went to every Sunday, of course. He was too embarrassed. I was the first of his kids, and his friends' kids, to start acting out.

The priest, my father and I sat on the hard wooden pew. The priest looked me in the eyes and asked question after question.

"Are you doing drugs, son?"

I wanted to laugh out loud, but I knew better. Did this priest really think that I would answer these questions honestly with my dad sitting right there? Somehow I knew, maybe the look on his face, that he wasn't buying it.

"Your son is not possessed. He's oppressed. The enemy is bearing down on his life, and your son is giving in." My dad didn't really understand what the priest meant, but he knew it was bad.

Just like everything else I enjoyed in my life, my mom wanted to stop this, too. Before I knew it, I was on a plane to Puerto Rico to spend some time with my grandma. My mom had never seen cocaine before she found my stash, and it scared the hell outta her. She thought that sending me away would clean me up. What she didn't realize is that where you go, your problems go. Heck, I didn't even regard it as a problem, let alone an addiction. All I knew was that I was having a good time, and there wasn't much that could stop me.

On the tropical island of Puerto Rico, I lay on the beach, soaking up some sun. It didn't get much better. New York had style, but Puerto Rico had beautiful tourists from all over the States.

That's when I met Beatrice. I went to a club and drank and danced. I got to know the party crowd rather quickly. With my experience in New York, I knew the lingo and the ins and outs.

"So who's got the good stuff?" I asked a new friend over drinks.

He gave me a crooked smile showing all his white teeth.

"Whatcha know about the good stuff, man?"

"I know enough. I'm from Manhattan, remember?" We laughed together, and he introduced me to some of his friends. Before I knew it, I was cutting lines with them nearly every night.

"Get up, Bernie," my uncle shouted. "*Levantense!*" I was startled from my sleep by his loud voice and the bright morning light streaming through the window. The digital alarm clock blinked 7:52. A headache quickly materialized around my eye sockets.

"What's going on?"

"You need to get up and eat breakfast."

"I'm not hungry."

"Listen, Bernie. You're going to eat breakfast, and then we're going to take you to the airport."

That woke me up. "What do you mean, airport? Who's coming?"

"Nobody's coming, you're leaving."

"I still have two more months here."

"No. We know what you've been up to. Your parents

sent you here to straighten you out, and you're here driving your grandma nuts."

"No, you gotta listen to me. I'll stop. Please just don't send me home."

"It's too late, Bernie. You're outta control. We bought the ticket already. Get your stuff together, and come to breakfast."

かかか

My dad stood up from the couch clutching a baseball bat. My mother sat next to him with tears streaming down her face. She looked like a mess. She started gasping for air like she couldn't breathe.

"What's going on here?" I was flying high, and the scene I walked up on didn't look right.

"Son, I gotta make a choice today. Your mother's just about lost it with your acting out. You're about to give her a nervous breakdown. So it's going to be you or your mother."

"Dad, what are you talking about?"

"Don't play dumb, Bernie. The drugs, the partying, we can't have that in our home anymore."

My brothers ran into the room and stopped dead in their tracks when they saw Dad with the bat in his hands.

"Dad, what are you doing?" Charlie shouted. His voice cracked, and I could tell he was about to start crying.

"Either you leave or I crack this bat over your head."

By this point, both of my brothers were bawling, and I

felt like doing the same. As much as I wanted to argue, I could see that he was right about my mom.

"Dad, you're going to throw out your baby boy?"

"I know this is hard, son, but you gotta leave. Don't even pack. We'll pack for you."

I kept in contact with Beatrice, and she convinced me to move in with her in California. The highway patrol was hiring, and I figured I could pass the test. I saw it as an opportunity. A second chance, even. I aced the test with no trouble, but I failed to show up the first day of work. I got a job with the post office and, again, failed to make it to the first day of work.

I don't know why I thought moving in with her would be a good idea. All I did was party and do coke. But even as much as she loved to party, the level of my drug use was higher than Beatrice could handle. She left me, and I met a new girl, Jenny. She stayed with me despite my daily drug use, and we had two daughters out of wedlock. I was snorting all our money, until I got to thinking, *If I sell blow, I could save some of the money I'm spending.* With the kids in the house, I kept things on the down low. I only sold what I had to, just enough to get by. Aside from that, I was my own best customer.

Jenny eventually got tired of it all, and she took off with the kids. I attempted to see them, but my drug-induced fog was thick. A combination of her anger toward me, my drugs and my stupidity kept me from my kids.

I liked doing coke, but I didn't like all the money I was spending. I was spending the rent money, the gas money, even my food money. So I kept selling coke, and before I knew it, the money got better. I started small but moved on up. The thrill of it had me hooked worse than the coke itself.

With my family gone, I got even more daring. Now I got deep into dealing drugs. Meeting up and making the sale, the danger, the beads of sweat and especially the rolled-up bills all gave me a kick I'd never gotten anywhere else. The more I sold, the more I made. *I could make a few hundred living like this,* I thought to myself.

As my sales got bigger and I got to know more people in California, I realized I could make thousands doing this. I didn't have to work some part-time job for minimum freaking wage. I could live big. There was no first day of work to miss. There was no uniform, no company policy manual, none of that. It was just blow and money. And girls. One after the other. I was hooked on every inch of it, and I was flying high.

One afternoon, I was sitting on my couch cutting up a nice fat line. I had already done about 12 grams that morning. I was about to bend down with my rolled bill when I heard shouting from outside. *Is it the cops? How did they find me?*

I inched over to the window and peered out from behind the curtains. I was suddenly drenched in sweat and felt dizzy. I fell to the floor and pulled my Beretta out from under the couch. *The snitches, man, they must have ratted on me.* I peeked out the window from my crouched position and spotted neighbors looking back at me from a window across the street. As I was staring out the window, my gun went off. I let go of the Beretta and fell onto my back. I was tangled in my clothes and panicking. There was a loud ringing in my ears from the gunshot. I'm not sure what happened next because the room was spinning rather fiercely. What I know for sure is cops busted in, and in my dizzy haze, I spotted SWAT in big white letters.

I came down from my high in a holding cell with a pounding headache. The ringing in my ears turned into throbbing. I tried to make sense of everything that had happened and realized that the majority of it had been hallucinations. I was flying so high that my own mind was playing tricks on me.

What was real was the cops busting into my apartment. They were onto me. Before I knew it, I was taking my belongings from a plastic bag and walking out of jail. I determined somehow God had spared me from the bulk of the trouble I could have been in.

Thank you, Diosito, I whispered while kissing the gold cross that hung on my chest. *Because you saved me from this mess, I'm not going to do coke anymore. I'm just going to deal.*

The second time the drug taskforce busted into my place, I snuck out the bathroom window and ran down the street. I was so deep into the life that not even another incident could stop me now. I didn't think I could want anything more than coke, but I could. I started using meth and hardly spent a waking moment sober. My new friend, meth, kept me up, up, up. I could feel the unnatural rhythm building in my heart. The beads of sweat on my brow and the undertow of anxiety filling my mind became constant.

By this time, the bright shining lights of my future were all dark. I lived at night now. In fact, I didn't sleep for 21 days straight. My thoughts became darker and darker. I couldn't go into my apartment without feeling like someone was watching me.

I'd come in and go straight to the fridge for a beer. *There's someone under the couch,* I thought to myself. *That's nonsense, nobody even fits under there,* I reasoned. *But I can feel their burning eyes watching me.*

Things went on like this, one day after the next. I couldn't have people over at times without stripping them down and checking for wires. New faces were possible cops, all the time. My heart beat faster, my brow sweated and the dark well of anxiety grew deeper.

After three weeks of sleepless nights, I finally fell back onto my bed and looked up to the ceiling. I couldn't keep my mind from reeling, but my body was burnt out. I pulled the gold cross from my sweaty chest and prayed, *Jesus, just take me in my sleep. Give me some kind of rest.*

It was hard to tell what was real and what was just the dope playing games with my mind. I knew my time was going to be up real soon because I could feel it in my abnormal heartbeat. I sensed that one person could only take so much anxiety before his heart just gave out. And despite my premonition, I kept sprinting full speed ahead just dealing, whoring, snorting, drinking and dancing. My mind was split in two because one moment I was drinking in the adrenaline of another sale, and the next I was praying, *Jesus, help me, just take me now.*

"Hey, man. Hook me up with some good stuff."

"Who is this?"

"Man, stop playing games."

"Well, what do you need?"

"I need 14 ounces of meth and 7 ounces of blow."

"That's a lot of dope. You sure about that?"

"Yeah, and meet me at the usual place." Of course I knew where to meet him.

"You sound a little funny. What's wrong with you?"

"Nothing's wrong. You gonna bring me the stuff or what?"

Even with the strange vibes, I couldn't turn down a sale. Something in my gut told me to play it safe this time. Usually, I walked around with a Beretta tucked in my waistband and a 22 down the back of my pants. But this time, I left them at home, and I didn't take all the merchandise he was asking for. I left the house in a T-shirt, shorts and slippers. I got in the car and drove to meet him at Montgomery Ward's.

"Go ahead and park where you always park," I heard him say on the phone. My stomach turned. As I pulled up to the store to park, I just had a bad feeling about the whole thing. I parked my car, and before I knew it, the muzzle of a gun was right in my face.

"FREEZE!" a cop shouted. "Put your hands on the steering wheel or I'll blow your head off." As I glanced over at the open police van, I saw my friend. I knew it was over. I got snitched on.

Anger surged through my veins as my knuckles went white clutching the wheel. But, at the same time, a strange feeling of peace washed over me. A voice deep inside of me whispered, *Finally, I get to rest.* I felt that rest take a hold of me, and my anxiety loosened. Another voice whispered, *It's okay. Now you're going to rest.* The cops yanked me from my car and handcuffed me. It was like watching a circus act as one after another exited a police van.

A cop walked right up to me and said, "Do you know how long we've been following you?" He shook his head in disgust and hawked a loogie right in my face. His snot ran down my nose and lips, and I could smell his hot breath. I was helpless, sitting with my hands behind my back.

"Listen, I'm handcuffed, officer. I'm not going to fight. Just do what you got to do, and take me in." They shoved me into the back of a cop car and tears ran down my face. Scenes from my childhood, my parents, my brothers all flashed through my thoughts. Memories of my daughters and happy times ran through my mind. I thought back to all the Christmases and Thanksgivings, holidays that I would never celebrate with them again.

Each day passed just like the day before as I did my time. I found out that if I went to program meetings, I could get a day taken off my time for each one. I went to my first meeting with an open mind. To my surprise, I started to enjoy the meetings.

Then I tried Alcoholics Anonymous and Narcotics Anonymous. I sat through the hour listening to one addict after another tell his story of ruin. *These guys are addicts.* They talked about shooting up and smoking rocks, and I somehow thought I was better than them. I didn't see myself as addicted.

Each week, I went back and sat and listened to men share their stories as they tried to piece together a new life in the correctional facility. I sat in the stark, windowless room in a metal folding chair. *I guess I can relate to these guys. Their stories are so similar to mine.*

With nothing better to do, I decided to attend church. Each weekend, I filed into the small chapel alongside other inmates. One particular Sunday, a minister from Oakland visited. He stood behind the pulpit preaching, and I was certain he was speaking directly to me. Either the cops told this guy about me, I figured, or my story got out.

His voice boomed, and he spoke with conviction. "You guys who don't serve God, and those of you who won't surrender your life over to him, are going to end up in hell."

A jolt of fear woke me straight up in the pew. After everyone left the chapel, I was stuck in my seat with his words resonating in my spirit. I sensed a voice call my name and say, *Bernie, kneel.*

I looked up at the ceiling, and I said, "God, Jesus, I know you are real, but I have no desire to stop using. If you are real, and I know you are real, I need you to take this desire from me because I know I am ruining my life."

Right then, I saw a bright white light shoot from the ceiling through my body. Again, I heard that same voice say, *Kiss the ground you are on because it is sacred.*

So I got on my knees, full of fear and humility, and bowed down and kissed the ground. I felt something dark and heavy lift from my life. All at once those bright stadium lights shone in my life again. I realized it wouldn't be my great skills that made my future but Jesus Christ alive in my life.

I wanted everyone to know that Christ was real, so I started telling one inmate after another about what happened to me. I woke up early on Sunday mornings and went to each dorm inviting inmates to church.

"There's nothing better to do here, just come with me to church," I said. Many guys looked up from their bunks and laughed in my face. They yelled obscenities and made vulgar jokes. I didn't care. These men needed to know Jesus was real and he cared about them. Sometimes nine or 10 would join me, and it made it all worth it.

One night, I lay awake in my bunk staring into the darkness. "What do you want me to do next, God?" I whispered.

I felt him say in my heart, *Read the Bible.*

"That's easy enough. Where should I start?"

In the book of Revelation.

"What? That's the scariest book in the Bible."

Yes. Read the Bible backward.

I finished the entire Bible — from Revelation to Genesis — two days before I got out.

"You're on fire now," the sheriff processing my paperwork said. "But the moment you hit the gates, you're going to leave that Bible behind just like the rest of them."

I stood at the bus station clutching my Bible and $500 in my pocket from my lawyer. It didn't faze me much that I was on a new track, but I had no family in California and nowhere to go.

"Where do you want me to go now, God?" I prayed while I sat on a bench watching all the travelers at the station.

I felt like God wanted me to join a program. I was confused because I'd already been clean for nearly eight months. I didn't think I needed the help of a program. But nonetheless, I listened to my heavenly father and called Diablo Valley Ranch. Four days later, I was bunked up in a room and on their schedule. I felt like I was incarcerated again, but I was okay with that. I listened to the staff, I went to meetings, listened to other addicts, read the NA and AA books — you name it, I did it all. I enjoyed the structure. It was really great getting to know myself and learning to love me again. I continued reading the Bible and incorporated daily reading into my recovery. Before I was done with the program, I had a weekly Bible study with three other residents. It was a pretty new thing for a resident to be reading the Bible with other residents in their free time. Reading and digging into God's word took us a step further in our recovery. It made such an impact, I was invited to come back and teach the Bible as an optional class.

One thing led to another, and I began taking courses to become an ordained minister. I was running full speed ahead, this time for the Lord and not myself.

One evening I was enjoying worship before a service. I was singing to God with my hands held high when I heard a woman say my name from behind. I turned around to see Claire, a girl I had dated during my addiction.

"I can't believe it's you," Claire said. "I saw your hands up in the air, and I knew it was you." I had run into her at a detox center a while before. I asked her if I could pray for her recovery. The first time she said no. But when I saw her the second time, she said, "Go right ahead." I could sense that God was working in her life, so I smiled. Seeing her there in church sure made my heart skip a beat. She looked happy and beautiful. She was on her own path to recovery, too.

Five months later, I was standing on stage for my ordination. Claire and her mom were in the crowd watching in amazement.

Neither of them could hardly believe that this hardened drug dealer was going to be a preacher. They started coming to my Bible study, and I married Claire one year later.

It was a blessing to help people through my ministry over the years. Watching God transform people's lives was a thrill that no drug could bring in my life. But I believed God wanted more out of me. It seemed like every time I turned around, he was stretching me.

One day I was sitting at a buffet enjoying the food. I

am a people person. So when someone passed by and made eye contact with me, I said hello.

"Good afternoon," said a man walking by with a group of people. He stopped in his tracks and turned around. "I don't know you, do I?"

"I don't think so," I said with a laugh.

"Well, God just spoke to me and said you are going to be my Hispanic pastor."

It was all the same to me. I already believed God worked in crazy ways, so I said, "That's fine, I do speak Spanish." I shook his hand and said, "God bless you."

"No, really, I mean it. You're going to be my Hispanic pastor."

We parted ways. Little did I know that two years later he would become my pastor. He mentored me and helped me take my faith in Christ to the next level. I guess you could say he became my spiritual father. In 2003, I started helping Pastor Jeff Kenney help men and women find more than just recovery. We help them find shelter, and New Hope International Church provides for their needs as necessary. For me, recovery was more than just getting saved. It was also about building lasting relationships.

❧ ❧ ❧

Claire and our five children have continued to support me in all I do. We've been on the same page in every way. Claire and I both found recovery through the combined power of programs and Jesus Christ. We needed Jesus to overcome addiction. But at the same time, programs provided structure and learning that we needed to really stay clean. The self-inventory that takes place, combined with the influence of the Holy Spirit working in a person's life, is powerful.

What started as three amigos reading the Bible together making their way to recovery eventually became an opportunity to preach onstage to a crowd of 350.

"Hello, my name is Bernie, and I am an addict. But today, I am addicted to Jesus Christ."

People stood and applauded. I looked out, and I saw a bunch of Bernies. I saw a whole bunch of people just like me. Before I used to think, *Those are drug addicts, and I am not.* I came to understand that we were all the same. We were all just a bunch of hurting people. There was nothing more special about me. I just decided to stand up and live my life for Christ.

His love and grace ran through me and into the crowd. I'd come to know a God who can restore lives. I prayed many others would come to know him, too.

ROAD TO FREEDOM
The Story of Victoria
Written by Rosemarie Fitzsimmons

I watched my parents disappear into the darkness as the night train pulled out of Cluj-Napoca station. I was almost certain I'd never see them again. They, of course, thought I'd be back in a week because my visa was only approved for a short visit.

All the documents I'd acquired over 30 years — my birth certificate and an electronics engineer diploma— were tucked into my shirt. These were not the sort of papers one took on a social visit. If anyone discovered them, I would surely be arrested and sent back.

I spoke to nobody in our small compartment during the three-and-a-half-hour ride. I listened to the *click-clack* rhythm of the wheels gliding along the tracks and stared out the window, taking in the sights and smells of spring as Romania's towns and villages flew past. Each time the train pulled into a station, my stomach churned with fear and excitement. Some people boarded, others got off and I'd exhale in relief as we left yet another town behind.

As the train neared Hungary's border, I dared to hope. I just might make it!

Then the train's brakes squealed, and we slowed, coming to a stop just before the border. Outside my window, armed police officers were entering and leaving a small building. A few leapt onto the train and began giving orders. One officer, who carried a large black baton, entered our compartment and shouted, "Everybody off! Take your luggage, and line up outside!"

I had only a small suitcase, which I grabbed from the overhead bin. I scurried out behind the others and took my place in a long line facing the train. The man with the baton started down the line, tapping people at random.

"You … you … you … go inside."

They'd grab their suitcases and enter the building to be searched.

Terrified, I looked only at the ground ahead of me. If he picked me, I was dead. I knew it. I could never in a million years explain those papers.

As he neared, I began to tremble, and I had to fight to appear calm. His steady steps approached, three people away … two … one …

"You!"

The baton hit the man on my left.

He was before me now. I would not look up. If he looked in my eyes, he would see my guilt. I held my breath and stared ahead.

His shoes turned toward me. The baton rose again.

"You!"

The baton hit the man on my right.

He'd passed me by.

The officer reached the end of the line, and everyone remaining returned to the train. We sat there for nearly two hours before the train finally gave a mighty hiss and pulled away. I exhaled for what seemed the first time since we'd stopped, and I looked around. Some of my traveling companions were missing, but others sat in their places — perhaps those who had been searched on an earlier train. Elated at my good fortune, I craned my neck out the window for my first glimpse of Hungary.

My first glimpse was a small building just over the border.

The train stopped again.

Again, officials stormed aboard, Hungarian police this time.

This time, I would not go unnoticed.

༄༅༄

My grandmother remembered a different Romania, a prosperous and free country, where area farmers supplied the cities with bountiful produce and Sundays were holy days. But by the time I was born in 1957, communist oppression gripped Romania. Most farms and all produce belonged to the government. Despite continuously high-yielding crops, the government exported nearly all produce to increase cash flow, leaving Romanians starving and fighting over the scraps. My city, Cluj-Napoca, was quite large, and its people suffered greatly.

To the starving, embittered people of Romania, God had become a myth, a fairytale. Most Romanians claimed to be atheists. Even in my own family, we only went to church at Christmas, more out of tradition than for religious reasons. In my heart, though, I knew about God because my grandmother talked of him.

One Christmas season when I was in second grade, my teacher asked the class, "Does anyone here still believe in God?"

I didn't hesitate and lifted my hand with confidence. Then I looked around the class. I was the only one. She made me stand up and began to ridicule me.

"How can you be so stupid? Who told you such foolishness?"

She berated me for so long, all the other children laughed.

Shame washed over me as I returned to my desk and sat down. I was still certain, but I kept it inside from that day forward.

I had no brothers or sisters. Mama worked in a factory, and Papa was a master shoemaker. They lived in good standing in our community because they knew how to act.

I learned how to act as well. I remember placing second or third in a fourth-grade poetry contest. Of course, all my poems were about the Communist Party, the communist leaders and the president. We treated our leaders like gods. We expressed love for them, and we praised them.

By age 7, I'd become comfortable being alone while my parents worked. I spent a lot of time behind our small one-bedroom house. I watched as people came in and out of the Pentecostal church next door. I heard them praying for each other, but they spoke strange languages that I didn't understand. I thought these people were crazy.

Despite my intense curiosity, I feared them. I believed they were evil.

When I neared the end of eighth grade, although I excelled at literature, I struggled in math — hated it, actually. I had a complex textbook and a terrible teacher. When I told my father I was in danger of failing the final exam (if you failed any part, you failed it all and could not advance to high school), he said, "If you don't pass, you will drop out and be put to work. You can go to school after."

My mother said, "You should still try, Victoria."

I tried to study, but I couldn't make sense of anything. Then one day, just before the test, I heard a small voice say, *You should pray.* I didn't know where the voice came from, but I argued with it.

"I don't know how to pray."

As I thought about it, I decided I had nothing to lose.

"God, I don't know math, but I want to pass this test, and I really want to go to school. I love school, but I just don't like math. Would you please help me pass the test?"

I took the exam, but I didn't think I did well at all. When the test scores were posted on the wall, I couldn't believe my eyes: I scored higher in math than in literature! In my shock, I jumped up and down, yelling, "I don't know how I did it!"

I came home and told my family God helped me. Everyone looked at me like I was nuts.

"It's a simple test," said Papa. "You were lucky. Forget about it."

But I couldn't forget.

One night, not long after that, a curious incident occurred that ensured I wouldn't forget. I was sleeping on my makeshift bed in the living room of our one-bedroom apartment. I woke in the middle of the night feeling two hands caressing my head from behind, touching me with such a great love. I put my hands up, thinking it was my mother, but there was nothing there. I looked back and saw the closed door to my parents' bedroom and believed it had been God. I had such a peace inside of me and a certainty that God loved me. I didn't know what to do with this feeling. I would need this certainty later, when it came time to flee the country, but at the time, I decided to push aside any thought of God.

ॐ ॐ ॐ

After high school, I had a desire to fight for justice and decided to become a lawyer. I believed that as a lawyer I could make the world right. To get into the class, I had to take another very difficult test that required us to memorize and recite speeches. I spent several hours a day studying communism, Marx, Lenin and other party leaders who wrote the speeches. I hated the speeches because they went completely against God. I could not memorize them, and I failed the test twice.

I decided to become a clerk.

At the technical school I attended, I was a good student. We went to school six days a week. The government kept us busy because they didn't want us to think for ourselves. We learned that Westerners were bad, evil people, and communists were the righteous ones. We didn't have newspapers anymore. Almost nobody left Romania, and foreigners were denied entry. So little information reached us from the outside world that we couldn't form our own ideas.

I didn't think much about the outside world because times were so hard. Our bellies were always empty. We didn't have toilet paper. Our hospitals lacked basic supplies, like syringes. People were dying in increasing numbers, particularly infants, many of whom died at birth. The government rationed bread according to family size. My family rated a half-loaf of old bread each day, so moldy it couldn't even be kept for a second day.

Stores closed. When the government decided to open the stores, we'd line up for whatever they had. People would take a chair or sleep on the ground all night long for a piece of bread, meat or fruit — whatever they held out, you took it. Because my parents worked, I stood in the lines.

All around me, people were angry, but not at God. What was God? To some people, it was just a dark word. There was no hope.

I remember walking with a group of young people, and we passed a mountain with a huge, ornate cross on it. The old cross came from a bygone era; I don't know why it hadn't been destroyed. When I saw it, all the hunger I'd witnessed through the years — all the death and despair and hopelessness — seemed to rush at me like a tidal wave. If God was real, how could he let these things happen? Anger overcame me, and I started shouting.

"Do you see this cross? This is a big lie!"

Everyone laughed. It meant nothing to them. I didn't have the strength to destroy the cross, but I wanted to. I was mocking God. My anger burned so fiercely, I felt as if it forced a crack in my soul.

❧❧❧

I received an opportunity to attend a one-year course in Bucharest that would lead to a job with an electronics company. One of my new roommates, Esther, introduced herself as a believer, but I didn't know what she meant. At first, I had flashbacks to the days I spent watching the Pentecostals, and I didn't want to get close to her.

Esther was nice and very wise for a 20 year old. She always helped me when I asked. In a short period of time, I learned to trust her wisdom. One night she had some friends over who offered to pray for us. Looking back, I believe their prayers helped sustain me later in my life.

I liked to read and would often bring home library books, which is probably why Esther gave me a Bible.

"It's hard to read," she said, "but you like to read, so it shouldn't be a problem. Start with the book titled John."

So I read. At first I hid the Bible from our other roommates and read only when they were out. I didn't want them to laugh at me like others had when I was younger. It got my attention right away, and I could not put it down. I wanted to read more, but they came home.

Every night we spent time together, laughing and talking. One night I said, "Girls, I want to read you something."

They said, "What is it?"

"The Bible."

"Oh, no!" They laughed.

"How about just a page?"

"No, just a half."

So I started to read. The intense quiet told me they were listening.

Then, all of a sudden, one girl stood and said, "That's enough. That's enough for today."

Still, they'd seen the Bible. I didn't have to hide it.

I kept talking with Esther. She invited me to one of her Christian group meetings on what happened to be my birthday, but I didn't tell her that. I bought some champagne, even though I didn't drink. I didn't have much of a social life at the time. All of my roommates drank and smoked and had relationships, but I did none of that. However, I wanted to make an exception on this special day.

On my birthday, I listened while the group prayed and sang and enjoyed it very much. When the meeting ended, I said, "Hey, today's my birthday, and I brought some champagne to celebrate!"

Everybody looked at me as if I'd dropped in from another planet.

"That's not good! Don't bring alcohol here. What are you doing?"

Their sudden turn stunned me. Once again, I felt rejected. They'd talked about love, but they didn't love me. I didn't understand.

I raced out, nearly in tears. *I'll never come here again.*

Later, Esther tried to explain that they rejected the drink, but not me. She said they wanted me to come back. I did not accept the invitation.

I tried another Christian group in another part of the city, but I had to take a bus to get there. I left late the first night, and I missed the bus home. I had to walk a long way in the dark. I've always been afraid of the dark and of dogs in the night. In my fear, I asked God to protect me, and I started to pray. On my own street, it was particularly dark, and dogs ran loose on both sides, all barking. Sure enough, some started chasing me. I raced to the house, but the gate was closed, and I had to jump over it. Surprisingly, they didn't bite me. I told the girls about the dogs and said, "God protected me."

They said, "Oh, here it is again, another story with God."

By then I was reading to them regularly from the Bible. In my excitement, I read them two pages that night. They weren't excited, but they let me read.

Esther and I worked in the same place, side by side, and became good friends. Again she invited me to her group, and I accepted. This time there were nice young people there, and I liked it, but eventually I stopped going.

Throughout my 20s, although I believed God was real, I felt as if he was always out of reach. I wanted to believe in him because there was nothing else left to believe in. I tried everything I could think of to experience him in a tangible way. I even listened to advice from my not-so-wise friend, Lydia.

"Victoria, you need to go to a fortune teller."

"A fortune teller, what's that?

"She can tell you things you don't know about your life and what to do about your future."

She took me into a dark and dirty home. An old woman greeted us, the smell of spices and mildew billowing around her as she moved. I didn't feel right about being there. She sat me down and started to talk.

"You've had a hard life, but soon you will meet a young person. He will be good for you, and you will marry."

She said nothing that couldn't be true for just about anyone, but I felt uncomfortable, and I wanted her to stop. She continued, her dark eyes staring right through me. I thought she was a devil.

"In order for this future to be released, you must say the rosary every night."

I rushed out and told my friend I would never go back again.

Yet, I said the rosary. We referred to it as the Mary prayer, which we said using beads. I said it every night. I started to have nightmares, and I would wake in a cold sweat. The nightmares were so bad that at one point whenever night approached, I would become fearful. I told Lydia about my nightmares, and she said I had to go back to the fortune teller.

Instead I went to Esther. She explained that this was not from the Bible because I didn't have peace. She prayed with me to be released, and I felt peace immediately. I stopped saying the rosary.

I resumed going to meetings with Esther. One evening after a meeting, I prayed, and I felt as if God said, *Open your heart to me, and I will listen to you.*

I remember crying and saying back, "God, if you really exist, show yourself to me." From that moment on, my life changed completely.

❧❧❧

"Victoria, do you want to accept Jesus?"

My heart fluttered. Since the moment Michael started speaking, I'd been captivated by his message of Jesus' love. Everything he said went straight to my heart. It felt right.

"Yes," I whispered. "But don't I need to be in a church?"

Beside me on the sofa, my friend Mirela looked frightened. She'd been as excited as I to come hear the missionary talk. They so rarely came to Cluj.

"No, we can do it right now, right here."

"Then, yes."

"Do you want to be baptized?"

"I can't. I'm not wearing white."

Wearing white mattered to me. I wouldn't budge on that. However, our host had a white dress in her closet. I tried it on, and it fit perfectly.

Mirela stood up, her face ashen.

"I have to go."

She left abruptly. I was too excited to chase after her.

Michael explained baptism more fully and said even Jesus himself had been baptized, by John the Baptist.

Excitement coursed through my heart. I wanted this.

We went upstairs to the bathroom, but when he turned the spigot, no water came out. At the time we were rationed to only two hours of water a day and cold water at that. So we waited. And waited.

Michael took me outside the group to talk. He asked me to remember from my early childhood any hurts or disappointments. I remembered a teacher when I was in kindergarten who had put me into the basement as a punishment. I remember crying and crying — it may have been only a few minutes, but to me it had been an eternity. Michael helped me forgive her and some others who had hurt me in the past. Then someone yelled that the water had come on, and we went back upstairs. I accepted Jesus into my heart and was baptized in ice-cold water. I felt as happy as could be.

❧❧❧

Esther met and married a young Hungarian man and left to live with him in Hungary. I felt so alone. I still went to meetings, but they weren't the same. I couldn't hang with the other girls — they were all nice, but we weren't the same. I decided to go to church.

I didn't go to the Pentecostal church close to my house because I remembered the strange meetings from my childhood. Instead, I started going to a Baptist church across town. It rained hard for five Sundays in a row, and I arrived at service each week soaked. Finally I said, "God, if it rains again, I'm going to the Pentecostal church." It rained again.

It was an old, traditional church, with strict rules about how women dressed: Scarves were mandatory, no jewelry, no makeup, no pants. I put on a scarf and left the house. My neighbor saw me in that scarf, and she said, "Hey, are you going to that Pentecostal church?"

Before long, I figured, everyone would know.

As soon as the preacher started to talk, I realized, *He's talking to me.* He was explaining the text I'd read in my Bible that week and answering all my questions. I started to cry. *This is the first time I've been here. How can he know me?*

The same scene unfolded week after week. I'd read my Bible and then go to church, and they'd be discussing exactly what I'd been reading about, and the teachers explained it well. Learning about God excited me. I wanted more. I enrolled in a prophecy class, but it was too hard to understand, so I decided to study by myself. I chose a book called Revelation, the last book in the Bible. A teacher named Daniel said with a smile, "You cannot start with this. When you go to school, you start in the first grade, then go to the second grade. You cannot start in high school. It's the same with God's book. Start at the beginning."

༄ ༄ ༄

I stood in the large meeting room on a Sunday, in front of all my co-workers and the company leadership. My co-workers were murmuring, speculating about my punishment as the manager began to chastise me.

"You know you have to work Sunday, this is what the law says. Why don't you come to work?"

I'd stayed home two Sundays in a row. Never mind that there wasn't much work to do. Attendance was required. I took a deep breath. It was time.

"I don't work Sundays, and I refuse to work Sundays."

The murmuring stopped; everyone froze, eyes and mouths gaped open.

"I don't understand," he said. "You don't have family, you don't have hardship, you're not sick …"

I looked him in the eye. "I'm a believer. I've accepted Jesus in my heart. Sundays are for God, and I refuse to work Sundays."

Shock exploded through the room. The leaders were clearly angry, and they turned to my boss, whose face contorted and changed color rapidly. I thought that if he could have killed me on the spot, he would have. "We'll talk about this later," he said, and he stepped out.

I never worked a Sunday again. Nothing ever happened to me. How's that for amazing?

❧❧❧

I'd been a Christian less than a year when I felt God tell me to leave. I didn't understand it, but I believed God was talking to me, day and night. I dreamt of going on a train, going on a bus, traveling long distances, meeting new people, talking in different languages. The dreams were delightful, but the reality seemed impossible.

I even felt as if God were with me at work. I couldn't help but be happy. It was as if he were laughing with me. I had a constant feeling that I was at a railway station, waiting for the train to leave.

Okay, I'm going to leave, I prayed. *Where shall we go?*

I felt him say, *To America, to California. Leave next summer.*

I believed I heard that clearly. Still, I couldn't help but think God was mistaken. I couldn't even get to the country next door. I did not know anyone in America. I had no money. The borders were closed. I could never get across.

The feeling would not cease. So I said, "Okay, if this is God, I'm going to take a step and see what happens." So, I would have to convince my boss, the same boss who wanted to strangle me over Sundays, to grant me an outlandish favor.

"Sir," I said, "could I have a week and a half off in one year's time?"

"Definitely not."

A few days later, I asked again. He said no. He said no four times.

On the fifth time, I asked, "Well, how about spring?"

"Spring? Maybe. When?"

"How about May?"

"Okay, May 1."

So, God came through! Well, then, I'll have to get a passport.

Most Romanians didn't own passports. The application process required getting past a lot of red tape, security approval, *many* signatures *and* $50 in your bank account. I had no money saved.

Although I was not in the Communist Party, I first needed Party approval to apply for the visa. The lady there who looked at my papers said, "Pshaw! This is ridiculous. You don't even have money. You have nothing."

I said, "Yes, but I still need your signature."

"You know what? When you have the money, come back, and I'll give you my signature." She flung the paper at me.

I said, "Okay, I'll do it."

Esther came to visit her parents, and I shared my story. She suggested I ask a friend of hers who lived in Holland for help. I wrote a letter, and Esther took it with her. A month later, I received a bank statement showing a deposit of 65 Guilders, which converted to more than $55. I marched right back to that Party representative and showed her the statement. She could not believe her eyes.

"Okay," she fumed. "Here is the signature, but you're never going to leave this country." She flung the paper at me again. I was too happy to care. For the first time, I accepted that if God wanted to take me out of Romania, no obstacles were going to stop him.

All the paperwork completed and all necessary signatures acquired, I brought my thick pile of papers to the police station to apply for the passport and visa. I presented my request and said I wanted to visit a friend. The official couldn't understand why I would want to go to Hungary. I said, "I just want to visit her. I've never been anywhere. I just want to go see her."

He pointed out that I had no assets, no house, no family, no money — no incentive to return. All that made me a terrible risk. Despite my rising fear, I insisted, "I'm just going to visit and come back." They said they would let me know.

A lady I knew came to me and said, "I heard you want to go to Hungry. They're not going to let you go. But I have a friend at the police station who can help if you pay him."

I went home and prayed. I felt sick about it. *I did not go through all these hoops for nothing. Now I'm to give this person money?*

I felt like God wanted me to trust only him. *He wouldn't have me bribe someone,* I thought. So I didn't pursue it.

I received my passport two weeks before I'd planned to leave.

ROAD TO FREEDOM

☙☙☙

I told my parents I was going to visit Esther. My heart broke to lie to them, but I couldn't trust anybody, not even them. I knew that out of love they would try to stop me. I also knew their reputation would be ruined, and they'd be put to shame by my actions. It was such a disrespectful way for a child to treat her parents.

Still, my excitement continued to build.

I had a scare at almost the last moment, when someone who identified himself as a police officer called and told me to report to the station the next day with my passport. Despite my fear, I prayed all the way to the station. When I arrived, they laughed at me and sent me home. I don't know what that was about, but it made the next week almost unbearable, knowing that at any minute something similar could happen again.

☙☙☙

At last, I was safely on the train, *click-clacking* along toward Hungary. I truly thought I was home free when we left the Romanian side of the border. I hadn't expected to stop again on the other side. I also hadn't expected the officer who entered our compartment to have a deep-seated hatred for all Romanians. It made sense, of course, because politically our two countries had been at odds often, particularly in recent years, which were rife with movements and uprisings. But I'd never witnessed the loathing firsthand.

The officer walked from one passenger to another, smiling politely as he checked passports. Then he stopped at my seat and looked at my papers. His face reddened, and he nearly shouted, "Where's your luggage?" I pointed up to the shelf. He pulled it down and flung it out to the walkway outside the cabin, all its contents in a pile on the floor.

I realized that because I was Romanian, he wanted me to give him a reason to make trouble. My temper flared, and I wanted to lash out, but I didn't. I took all my emotions and stuffed them into my chest and started picking up my items. He stomped off, and I returned to my cabin. The train began to move again. Now I was truly free.

We arrived in Budapest in the morning. Esther was two hours late picking me up. I didn't know a word of Hungarian, so I nearly became despondent waiting for her. I didn't know what to do. When I saw her, I raced to hug her. "Oh, Victoria, you're not going to go back, yes?"

"No, never."

I settled in for a while with Esther and her family (she'd recently had a baby). By the middle of June, she'd helped me find a job at an agriculture institute. I'd brought my papers to the immigration office, where they were translated into Hungarian. The only obstacle was I didn't speak the language. Esther spoke for me. The engineer who examined my certificate said everything looked good. I showed up the next day and started working.

Hungarian is nothing like Romanian, it's closer to Italian. Initially, I learned two key phrases: "I do not speak Hungarian" and "What is this?" Those phrases got me through the first three months. When I'd get a task, I'd just say, "What is this?" and they'd show me what to do.

I worked hard to learn their language. It took me three months to open my mouth and have an actual conversation.

Eventually they said I spoke as well as the foreign students at the nearby university. I was so happy there. I even got an apartment. I felt like God was reminding me to get to America, but I ignored him until the day Esther stopped in for a visit.

"So, why aren't you continuing on?"

"I don't know. I'm waiting."

"Do you think someone is going to show up on a white horse and take you there?"

"You know what? God can do that. Right now, I'm waiting."

"What are you waiting for?"

I didn't know. She was right. It was time to go on my next leg: to Holland, the only other place where I knew anyone. I contacted the woman in Holland who had sent me the money, and she replied that she'd provide a place to stay if I could make it there.

Hungary was also a communist country, and I wouldn't be permitted to cross the border freely. My visa was for Hungary only and had long since expired. I would have to sneak out.

Esther knew a missionary friend in Holland named Lucas who smuggled Bibles into Hungary and Romania using Christian tour groups as a cover. He stashed Bibles in a secret compartment in the luggage bay under the bus. Esther contacted Lucas, and the next time he came to town, he called for me to meet him in a nearby hotel lobby. I worried about going to him because I didn't know him. I worried it might be a trap.

We talked in the lobby. Lucas was nice, and he spoke English. I'd studied English in Romania and spoke it well.

He said, "Can you spin around?"

I understood his words, but they didn't make sense to me.

He said, "Spin, like a ballerina."

So I twirled in front of him, until he said, "That's good."

He sent me home, saying, "Show up here, tomorrow night."

I packed a small bag with my papers, a few pairs of underwear, an extra shirt and my Bible, and I said goodbye to my small group. We prayed for a safe journey and for miracles.

Lucas met me at the hotel and brought me to his room. He left me, saying, "I'll be back shortly," but he was gone a long time. When he returned, he smelled like alcohol. He sat on the bed and said, "Come sit next to me."

This is not good.

"No, I'm going to sit here by the door."

Furious and frightened, I looked from the door to

Lucas. I don't know where the strength came from, but I yelled, "Leave me alone!"

Lucas roared, and I ran for the door. Then, as if he'd flipped a switch, he changed his demeanor.

"No problem, no problem," he said. "I'm sorry. We won't talk of this, okay? I will get you there. I'm sorry. I'll be back at 4, and I'm going to take you to Holland."

I calmed down, but I worried because I had no way to protect myself. In the morning, Lucas was a different man. He explained his plan, which was to put me in the secret Bible compartment. That's why he'd had me spin around — to see if I'd fit. He led me to the bus and showed me a coffin-like metal box behind the luggage section. When closed, it just looked like the back of the bus. I climbed in, and he slid the door shut, leaving me in utter darkness.

"When you hear loud steps, you will know you are safe," Lucas said. "Until then, stay put."

I had to lie on my back on the hard metal, which hurt my spine. If I'd been only a bit taller, I wouldn't have fit. I could barely move my fingers. People started packing luggage, making a lot of noise. I lay there about an hour just waiting to leave.

So that's how I left Hungary, one year after I'd arrived. We rode for five or six hours, but for me it felt like an eternity. At first I fared all right, but after a while, I almost couldn't bear it. Not only did I want desperately to move, but metal rods on either side of me became very hot. Terrified, I started to cry, but almost immediately the fear left me. I remembered God and felt he was there.

We stopped several times, and the bus would shake above me as people moved about.

Once I thought I heard officials inspecting the luggage area and thought, *Perhaps we're on the border?* After what seemed like a very long time, the bus resumed its journey.

We stopped again, and I heard the loud steps, a knock and then the most wonderful words: "Okay, you're safe. You can come out."

I was hungry and thirsty but all right. Lucas stared at the ground. The tourists had left the bus, and we were alone.

"We've crossed the border, and we're in Austria," he said. "I had to let you out to make sure you're okay, but I have bad news. I cannot take you farther. There's no way to get you back in the box unseen. I can't risk it."

"You promised!" My heart raced. "I don't know anyone in Austria. They're going to send me back, and I cannot go back. I don't know what they'd do to me if I got sent back. You promised to take me to Holland!"

He shook his head and sighed and then had an idea. He told me to walk around until all the passengers were back in their seats and then approach the bus and pull him aside. Then he would get on the bus and tell them I'd asked for asylum in Holland and ask if they'd allow me to travel with them. If even one of them was not comfortable with the plan, then he would not take me. I said, "If that's what I have to do, I'll do it." So I stepped out and waited.

Austria is beautiful, but in my shock and fear, I could not really admire it. Finally, the tourists boarded the bus, and I approached as Lucas instructed. He made me stand beside him at the front of the bus and took the microphone. In English, he explained that I was a Christian and I wanted to cross Germany and go to Holland, but they all had to agree.

Hands flew up all the way down the aisle. Some of the believers in the back stood and clapped. The bus burst into cheers. They were so nice. Some called me to come sit with them. They offered me food.

We stopped in Germany at a very nice hotel in the mountains. The believers from the bus gave me so much food, I couldn't eat it all. I said I liked ice cream, although I'd never had it. They brought me a giant glass bowl filled with the delicious treat, topped with chocolate sauce and sprinkles. I was amazed, but I could only eat half of it.

The next day, our bus approached the checkpoint at the Holland border. Lucas warned us that the officials might come aboard to check passports, so I prepared to hide, crouching near the back. It was a scary moment, but they did not stop us.

Finally, we arrived in Holland, in a cold, windy downpour. I wore only a light shirt and wasn't sure what to do. One of the ladies said, "Last stop. Let's get off. Where's your coat?"

I said, "I don't have anything."

She looked at me and then took off her jacket, a nice jacket, and gave it to me. I wore that coat for the rest of my stay in Holland.

Lucas took me to his home. Then I stayed for a few

weeks with a lady I'd met on the bus. Eventually, I had to report to the authorities, who sent me to a refugee camp for four and a half months.

At the refugee camp, I filed a request to go to America. I met other Hungarian refugees while in the camp, and when it was time, the five of us went together to request asylum. The others went first — they were turned down. Political asylum could not be granted to refugees from Hungary. With tears in my eyes, I put my papers down on the table and said, "I'm from Romania, not Hungary."

So I was granted political asylum, and my new friends went back to Hungary. It took another year and four months to complete the process and get a green card. I located the woman who had put money in my bank. She had just had a baby and wanted company, so she let me stay with her to help until I left.

Among my many new challenges, I had to come up with the money to pay my fare of $850, I had to pass health exams and obtain the proper medical forms (and pay for all those) and go to an interview in Belgium to speak with the American consul for emigration. Lastly, I had to find an American sponsor.

The church I went to helped me pay for the physical and helped me get to Belgium. While there, I met a man who scoffed at my story.

"Wake up. You can't get to America. Who's going to help you? You don't even have money to buy your ticket."

All questions I'd asked myself. But I would not be swayed.

"I have God."

"God won't pay for your ticket."

"I know that, but I believe he will help me."

He shrugged, left and then came back with an address.

"Write to these people. They help those in need. Ask them for money for the plane."

I'd never heard of a place like this that helped people in need. I went back home and wrote. It was a Catholic organization, and someone soon contacted me by letter.

They agreed to pay my fare but said I had to report to them as soon as I got there. They warned me that making my way would be hard, particularly at first, but asked me to pay them back as soon as I found work — $10 per month. I was okay with that because then they could help someone else the way they offered to help me.

I had everything taken care of except a sponsor family to help me through the first months. Out of the blue, I remembered Michael, the missionary who'd baptized me with the cold water. He lived in Sacramento, California. I wrote to him, and he said yes, he'd sponsor me.

I arrived in America on October 25, 1992. Michael and his family greeted me with a cake, saying, "Ah, it's the girl in the box!"

I felt so grateful and so happy, no words can describe it.

While at the migration center in Sacramento, a woman asked me nicely where I would start work. When I said I had no idea, she reached into her purse and pulled out $100.

"Here," she said. "Welcome to America."

Almost immediately I found work, and I sent the Catholics $10 per month until I paid off the debt. I liked to say, because of God and Catholics, I'm in America.

I met and fell in love with a young man. His first wife had passed away of heart disease at 28, and he had three small children. In fewer than eight months, we married, and we raised his children together.

My husband was ordained as a pastor by the Pentecostal Church of God, and in 1998, we had an idea for a mission trip back to Romania and Hungary.

Communism had been abolished there for nearly a decade. We posted a request on our Web site for baseball gloves to bring to the youth in Europe, teach them a new game and present the Gospel to them.

Pastor Jeff from New Hope International Church responded to our request and provided many gloves, which we packed into our suitcases. Our endeavors were successful in Romania and Hungary.

And so began our relationship with New Hope. We felt such love there, we joined the church right away.

❧❧❧

I waited in the baggage area of Oakland International Airport, watching hundreds of travelers swarming in different directions. I searched the crowd for familiar faces. *Had they made the flight?*

We'd been corresponding for about three years, since

the Romanian Revolution, which brought an end to the communist regime and opened the country to the outside world. Once or twice, I'd even managed a phone call.

Now they were coming here for an entire year. I could barely contain my excitement. They would get to spend time with my husband and our three precious children, who we were raising with God's grace.

With a loud *clang*, the baggage carousel began to move. Travelers crowded its perimeter as luggage began shuffling past. I noticed their clothes and could tell which people were arriving by their long dark skirts and woolen suits. Change would come, but gradually.

Then I saw her, older than I remembered, but with a gaily colored scarf on her head and a familiar sparkle in her eyes.

"Mama?"

I ran to her and was caught up in a hug I'd never thought I'd feel again. Papa, returning from the carousel with a small valise in each hand, dropped his bags and held his arms wide. I ran to him, praising God that I should be able to see him again.

They never learned of my trials. They only knew that I had made it to America, that I loved God with all my heart and that, finally, I was truly free.

ADRIFT
The Story of Orin and Pearl
Written by Arlene Showalter

Orin

"I got no home." I scowled and crossed my arms.

"What do you mean by that?" My sister Cassie tried to put one arm around my shoulders. I ducked away.

"Nobody wants me. You know that. I know that. Your dad. My dad. All the other 'dads' Mom's brought home. They don't want me."

"I want you."

"You have your own life. Besides, you've already shipped me off to Dad once. Remember?"

"Only because you refused to listen to reason." Again, she reached out to touch me. I stepped to the lake's shore, selected a stone and sent it skipping across the still water.

I've got the world by the balls, man. I don't need you or anybody else trying to tell me what to do. The lake swallowed the pebble. I squared my shoulders and faced Cassie square on.

"I can take care of myself."

"How? You're only 15." She lifted both hands in a helpless gesture. I slapped mine on my hips.

"Go back to your life, and let me get on with mine."

❧❧❧

"You're adopted," teased my half-brother Mike, older than me by four years.

"Am not."

"Are, too. Look at your big head. You're some sort of Mongoloid kid. You got switched at the hospital."

I slunk outside and wrapped my skinny arms around my knees, which projected at an awkward angle from my body. *Maybe Mike's right. I don't look like anybody, not even Mom.* Heavy thoughts for a 6-year-old kid.

❧❧❧

"I need to talk to you." My oldest half-sibling, Cassie, rounded up her full sister and brother and me — the oddball with the different dad. "Mom's going away."

"Why?" Mike asked.

"She's a little sick. She'll only be gone a few weeks."

"What about us?" I asked.

"We're going to stay with Uncle Dan and Aunt Lucy."

"What about Wayne? Where's he going?" At age 8, I liked my latest stepfather who treated me as a blood son. He coached me in baseball and took me fishing.

Our house rang with love and laughter until he and Mom drank. Then, like volcanic eruptions, the lava flow of drunken anger incinerated and consumed all the good times. So, Wayne exited our lives, and we four kids moved into Uncle Dan and Aunt Lucy's house.

It can't be too bad. Cassie said Mom will be back in a couple of weeks. I can handle that. I settled in for the short stay.

The contrast of life in their home hit as hard as an Eskimo dropped off in the Sahara, but I quickly adapted to the unconditional love they both expressed to all of us. Uncle Dan and Aunt Lucy opened wide both their home and hearts to us.

We all sat together for family dinner every night. We enjoyed board games together. Never once did we witness the drunken brawls so common in our own home.

After two years of living with them, I'd almost forgotten what Mom looked like.

Even though I appreciated the respite from all the chaos that seemed to always surround her, I wondered how she could abandon her four children for so long.

I strolled to school one morning, deep in these thoughts. Suddenly I heard the *toot-toot* of a horn as a car pulled up and stopped beside me.

"Hi, Orin. Want a ride?" Mom smiled from the passenger seat.

"Mom?" I strove to hide my shock while studying the strange man gripping the steering wheel.

"Hop in." She twisted around and opened the rear door.

"Okay." Mom turned the other way and tapped my knee. "How're you doing, Orin? You look good."

I could only nod. *Who is this guy, and why is he driving Mom around?*

"This is Arthur."

Can Mom read my mind? I glanced out the window before pulling my eyes back to meet Mom's happy gaze.

"I call him Art. He's your new dad."

Art and Mom moved Mike and me from Washington to California. Cassie had married, and my other half-sister had moved on as well.

Soon, familiar shouts, thuds and curses rang through the house. As soon as liquor entered my parents' bodies, reason fled their minds.

"Orin, get up right now." Mom shook my shoulder as I slept not long after our move.

"What? What?" I jumped out of bed in a panic. *Is the house on fire?*

"Pack your bags. Right now."

What? I knuckled my sleepy eyes. *What is she talking about? What time is it? What's going on?*

"Hurry up." She gave me an impatient push. I began slapping clothes into the bag she'd flung open on my bed. As my mind crawled toward wakefulness, I remembered the latest fight the night before.

As usual, I could detect no real reason. As soon as the two got saturated in booze, the usual curses, punctuated by screams, filled the air and fists pummeled the walls — and more.

Just as I put my hand on the knob to the front door, Mom touched my shoulder. "It's so late. Let's wait until morning."

I crawled back into bed. A few hours later, the alarm rang for school, and I stumbled toward the kitchen with apprehensive steps.

What kind of condition is Mom in? Art?

"Good morning, Orin." Mom smiled as she sipped from a mug of coffee.

"Hey, kid," Art added. "How ya doing?"

What the heck? A few hours ago, we're fleeing the scene. Now Mom looks like June Cleaver, all tidied up, calm and smiling.

Angry and confused, I mumbled, "Okay."

"Here's your cereal." Mom put a bowl, spoon and box in front of me. "Enjoy."

"Thanks." I stifled a yell and kept my balled fists out of sight.

అఅఅ

"Why do you stay with him?" I demanded a year later, when I was 11.

"I don't need your lip." Mom scowled at me. "Maybe it's time for you to go to your real dad." She threw some quarters on the table and thrust a paper at me. "Here's his number. Now get out of here and call him."

I dragged myself to the payphone in the park. I stared long and hard at the number before dropping the required number of quarters into the slot with shaking hands. *I don't even know my dad. How's he supposed to know me?*

"Hello." The stranger's voice filled my ear.

"This is Orin." I tried to keep my voice steady, but fear made me cry.

"Hello. Hello? Who is this?" Dad repeated.

I cried harder, unable to get out any words.

"Is this a crank call?" Irritation crept into my yet-unknown father's voice.

I hung up the phone and hid myself nearby in a deep patch of ivy. *I don't want anyone seeing me crying like a baby.* I lay there for some time. *He doesn't even know who I am.*

Minutes, or hours, passed. I lay as still as possible when I heard footsteps approaching, receding and approaching again.

"Orin?"

Go away! I pressed my body down deeper into the ivy.

"Orin?" Cassie's voice turned insistent. "I know you're around here somewhere, so you may as well show yourself."

I crawled out of the ivy, hoping she'd miss the proof of my tears.

"What's wrong, Orin?" She stepped closer and touched my wet cheek. "Why were you hiding?"

"Mom made me call Dad. He didn't even know me."

"I'm sorry." She put a hand on my shoulder.

"Nobody wants me."

"That's not true. You have Mom. And me."

᭪᭪᭪

Mom and Art moved to another town in California. Mike moved on in his life. Cassie moved east with her husband, Josh, and baby girl. That left me alone in a house with the drunken duo.

Another in their endless series of fights escalated until I caught Art straddling Mom on the floor and punching her in the face. I threw a punch of my own and knocked him off her. Murder raged in my heart as I swung again.

A neighbor heard the commotion and called the police. They arrived and defused the situation.

"Ma'am, was your husband beating you?"

"No, no," she insisted, shielding her battered face. "I just fell."

"You're lying," I said, brave in the presence of official authority.

"No, I am not."

"How old are you, son?" One officer turned to me.

"Twelve."

"You say your dad was beating up your mother?"

"Yes, and he's not my dad. He's my stepdad."

He turned back to Mom.

"He's lying," she repeated.

"Sorry, ma'am, but your son seems to have no reason to lie. We're taking you to a safe house — right now."

"Is there anyone you can call?" the supervisor asked Mom at the shelter.

"Only my daughter. But she lives in Tennessee."

҈ ҈ ҈

Cassie invited us to stay with Josh and her, so we made the move across the country.

"Mom wants to go back to California," Cassie told me a few months later.

"To *Art*? You serious?"

She nodded her head.

I shook mine. "I can't go back. I'm afraid of him."

"I understand. We don't want you to go back there, either. You can stay with us."

Without a misstep or backward look, Mom signed away all her rights, releasing her son to her daughter before returning to Art.

৵৵৵

A stranger to my biological father, abandoned by my mother and several stepfathers and frightened by my current stepfather, I felt unwanted, unloved and unneeded. The void drove me to hang out with the rough kids down the street, looking for family, acceptance and value.

Everyone smoked weed, so I joined in. Everyone drank, so I embraced the very liquid that poisoned my own family and life. They all experimented with hard drugs, so I did, too.

"You need to stop," Cassie said one night when I stumbled in the front door and fell on the living room floor. "You are killing your future. If you don't stop, you're going to wind up dead."

I shrugged and staggered off to my bedroom.

Other times I returned to Cassie's home, high on PCP.

"Orin, please," she begged. "We don't want the cops banging on our door, telling us they found your body in a ditch. Please think about what you are doing."

"I don't need you or anybody else telling me what to do." I stomped out of the house and down to my friends' homes. *These guys are my real family. They care about me. They've got my back.*

A few weeks later, as I reeled down the street, high on PCP and drunk as a skunk, a car pulled up to the curb and stopped.

"Hop in." Josh threw open the passenger door.

Whatever. I climbed in.

I awakened the next day when I felt someone shaking my shoulder. "Huh?" I sat up and looked around. *What the heck?* I looked up into the face of a uniformed stranger standing over me.

"Here." He handed me $10. "The guy who dropped you off at the Greyhound station yesterday gave this to me. He says to give it to you to buy some dinner."

Greyhound station? Money? Food? What's going on? Where am I?

"We put you on this bus last night," he explained. "But this is as far as you go on this line. If you'll follow me, I'll show you where you need to transfer."

Transfer? I followed like a confused lamb. *To where?*

He handed me a ticket. "You're going to Seattle." We walked a few more paces. "Here's the bus you need to be on."

The bus rolled into Seattle. I saw a worried-looking man scanning the passengers as we disembarked the bus.

"Orin?" He stepped forward as my feet touched Washington ground again.

"Yes."

"I'm your dad. I'm here to take you home."

❧❧❧

"You need to get your son school clothes," Dad's girlfriend, Lacy, told him.

"I do?" Dad's blank stare proved he had no clue how to raise a son about to enter the ninth grade.

"He needs to be enrolled, too."

"Oh."

"I'll do it." Lacy smiled at me. "It'll be fun."

Dad worked in sales and drank up his commissions. I hated the confined quarters of his dinky studio apartment, so I began hanging out at the nearby park. Trouble followed me like a Labrador retriever.

This is a waste of time. I stagnated in school. Restless, I began cutting class and spending more time with my new rough friends. Danger stimulated me.

❧❧❧

Where am I? I opened my eyes and saw white. Lots and lots of white. White ceiling. White walls. White sheets and blanket. I tried to turn. *Ouch.* My left arm refused to turn with me. My bleary eyes traveled to my elbow, then my forearm, then my wrist. *What the — heck?*

My wrist was shackled to the bed. The bed had rails. *Rails?*

"Glad to see you're awake."

"Cassie?" I croaked. "What are *you* doing here?"

"Your dad called me because he hasn't seen you for months." She frowned. "He had no idea if you were dead or alive. At least this little caper brought you back into the family radar."

"I have a few questions." I stared up at a strange man standing over me. *Oh, crap. The fuzz.*

"You were in a gang-related fight." He motioned toward my bandaged wrist. "One guy decided to rearrange your face with a broken bottle. Your block saved it." He grilled me, determined to get more details about the fight.

I knew the price of ratting out — especially with gang members. *They're a bunch of bad dudes. I ain't talking.*

"We can only release him to his guardian, ma'am. Do you know who that is?" He turned to Cassie.

"I'm still his guardian. I'll make sure he gets home to his father."

A few days later, Cassie and I visited the park near Dad's apartment. She tried to help me formulate a plan for my future. I tapped my foot and yawned.

"Look at you, Orin. You're only 15. You could've been killed. Whatever possessed you to get involved with a gang? You're walking down a dead-end street with all this partying and fighting and drugs and drinking. It's going to kill you."

"So? Nobody cares what happens to me."

"That's not true. You know I do."

"You have a life. You have your own family. You don't need me screwing it all up for you. I'm not your problem."

"I'm still your guardian."

"Well, you shouldn't be. Where's Mom been all these years? And Dad? They just dumped me off onto you because they don't care. I don't have a home. I don't have a family. And, *I don't care, either.*"

Cassie stood to walk back to Dad's place. "We'll discuss this later."

"Nothing to discuss." I flipped a rock into the lake and stomped off.

ംഴംഴംഴ

"I'm here to take you back to your mom." Art stood at Dad's door a few days later.

"What?"

"Your sister Cassie called me to come get you, so here I am."

Tension filled the car and scorn filled my heart on the long drive from Seattle to Northern California.

"Things are different now," Art promised. "I haven't touched your mom since that night."

I turned and looked him square in the eye. "If you *do* touch her, I promise I will kill you."

Mom and Art still drank and fought — but he remembered to keep his fists to himself. She finally left and divorced him and quickly found another man.

Oscar treated Mom and me with respect, but he shared the same similarity to all Mom's choices — the love of the bottle.

I returned to school, only to quit again in the 11th grade. The pull of drugs and desire for freedom to control my own life proved too much. I moved out on my own and into the deadly world of dealing and doping.

ॐॐॐ

Pearl

"You have to stop drinking!" Mama's voice penetrated the walls deep in the night. I snuggled deep under my blanket and pretended to sleep, but my 3-year-old heart pounded with fear. By my 5th birthday, Mom left Dad. She moved around for a while with my brother Dylan and me until she found an affordable place and took three jobs to support us.

"Keep an eye on your sister," Mom said as she dashed off to one of those jobs.

"Yeah, yeah."

Two minutes after her departure, 11-year-old Dylan sprinted toward the front door. "See ya."

I sat alone in our living room, too scared to cry. I flipped on the TV and clutched my blankie.

Bam! A 6-year-old imagination travels quick and far. *What was that?* My heart pounded while I listened. I stood on shaky legs and followed a steady humming sound into the kitchen. A few minutes later, *bam!* I watched the refrigerator lurch into silence.

Even knowing the source of the noises, I jumped every time it switched on and every time it switched off. My nerves developed a sensitivity of their own, constantly jumping and twitching at every unknown source of sound.

Dylan seemed to know Mom's schedule and always slid into the house slicker than a San Francisco Giant heading for home.

I kept my mouth shut. I always kept my mouth shut.

A few months after our move, Dad showed up. He looked around. "Where's your mom?"

Dylan came out of his bedroom.

"What are you doing here?"

"I'm here to see Pearl. Where's your mother?"

"Working."

"In that case, I'm taking Pearl on a little adventure."

"You're not allowed." Dylan took one step forward.

"You plan on stopping me?"

Dylan stepped back. "I'll tell Mom," he whined.

"Go ahead." Dad shrugged and took my hand. "Tell her we're going to check out Reno."

As we rode the Greyhound bus, I watched the desert roll by and reveled in this time alone with Dad. *I love him so much.* Too young to understand why moms and dads no longer live together, I did comprehend why Mom insisted he stop drinking.

Booze made him crazy and very, very unpredictable. But asking questions as to why he continued drinking was out of the question, so I sat back and enjoyed the ride.

"Can you watch my little girl for a while?" Dad handed some bills to a woman in a Reno casino restaurant.

"Sure can." She tucked the money into her corset and crossed her legs. I marveled at the height of her heels and short, short skirt as I hopped onto the opposite bench.

She chatted in a friendly way as Dad moved on to some strange machine. He moved a handle up and down with one hand and held a drink in the other.

Hours passed. My eyes got heavier and heavier, and I finally slumped down on the restaurant bench and slept.

The next day, Dad and I strolled down the sunny sidewalks of Reno. He began calling everyone he knew, trying to pilfer money off of someone, anyone, to get more booze. The cops drove up while we sat on a curb. They saw Dad was already teetering with alcohol.

"We're running you in for public intoxication." One officer bent toward me and studied my arms, covered with small red blotches. "And maybe even child abuse."

"Sorry, sweetie, but we have to take you into foster care for three days," one cop said, "to make sure this man is really your dad and hasn't harmed you."

A kind lady put me to bed in a room with other children. Even though she seemed nice, I couldn't sleep. Instead, to keep from panicking, I concentrated on a snowy mountain of socks she'd left for sorting and folding the next day.

"Oh, dear, what's this?" the lady asked the next morning when she discovered more red blotches, which I kept scratching. "I think you have chicken pox!"

The police released me to Mom as soon as she arrived.

After the Reno police released Dad, he stayed at a Salvation Army shelter and worked on putting his life back together. He visited me often and each time brought a huge stuffed animal purchased at the Salvation Army thrift store.

One day, just as third grade let out, I spotted him walking toward me, my handsome Hulk Hogan look-alike daddy, with the gorgeous blond hair and sunglasses. In his arms he carried a gigantic stuffed teddy.

My dad's the coolest. He'd stayed sober and moved into a small place directly behind our house. He got a respectable, responsible job. Life smoothed out.

Then I met Cherry.

❧❧❧

We both rode the same bus to high school. She penetrated my keep-quiet-and-to-myself exterior with her quick grin and laughing eyes. We became friends, and I visited her home.

My dad looked cool, but her parents *were* cool. Both drank — a lot. I often stayed the night.

"Come on," Cherry whispered after her parents retired.

"What?" I stifled a giggle.

We snuck to the den. Cherry opened the liquor cabinet and reached for two glasses.

"Your parents will know when they check the bottles," I fretted.

"Not to worry. I'll refill them with water."

Liquor transformed me. I felt prettier, funnier, even smarter.

Cherry also taught me how to shoplift cigarettes from the counters of our local convenience stores.

"Can I celebrate the New Year with Cherry's family?" I asked my mom. "We're going to watch old movies together."

"Sure. Go and have a good time."

I got falling-down drunk and called my dad the next morning for a ride home. He never said a word, but his silence made me know that he knew what I hoped he didn't know. Both my parents preferred to address issues through silence rather than address and solve them.

"Here, take a drag of this." Cherry held out a reefer, encouraging me with her irrepressible grin. I took a long drag, and for the first time in my 16 years, my body relaxed. The mute tension of living with a mother who worked non-stop and a brother who resented being tossed into a responsible role at 8 years old evaporated in a cloud of weed. I rested my head on the back of the sofa and closed my eyes, savoring the unexpected, foreign calm.

In our school, drugs sprouted quicker than dandelions, and everyone seemed to sample them. Acid sheets cost a mere $2, easily affordable because of my afterschool job.

Acid took me outside myself. It gave me an escape from what *was* to what I imagined. I liked the "me" it created in my mind. A "me" I could live with. A "me" who felt successful and grand.

Drinking to oblivion made me forget who I was and who I wasn't. I never controlled it, nor had any desire to. I drank until blackout released me from reality.

One morning, I awakened on the couch of a strange home.

Where am I? I wondered, rubbing my aching temples.

"Hello, is anyone home?"

Silence.

I began walking from room to room, looking for someone to solve the mystery as to where I was and how I got there. Finally, I found some mail lying on a desk. *Now I have an address. I can call a cab now.*

My class clique moved on to meth. We congregated in the school lavatory and did lines behind closed, locked doors. Meth helped me work two jobs and study for finals as high school graduation approached. I accomplished it all while sleeping one night a week.

I moved on to junior college and dealing meth at the same time. What I didn't sell, I used. One day I came home and discovered my pot-weighing scale was missing.

Oops, Mom must have found it. I waited for an explosion from either parent. None came. Rather than confront my business and life choices, Mom simply removed the scale — and kept silent about it.

I decided to move in with a friend. *Who needs their wordless disapproval?* I continued dealing and using.

❧❧❧

What is this? I awakened on my mother's couch a year later. *How did I get here? Why am I here?*

I looked at my feet. *Hospital booties? What the heck?*

Mom walked in the room.

"What's going on?" I demanded. "Why am I here, and why do I have these awful things on my feet?"

"You have no idea?"

"Idea of what?"

"You don't remember being in the hospital?"

"No." Annoyance tinged my voice.

Mom studied me. "Your friend's mother saw you lying unconscious in the stairwell where you live, behind a locked door. She called the paramedics, who broke down the door and rushed you to the hospital."

"She did? They did?"

"Yes. Your father and I came to get you, and the nurses said you screamed all night. And, apparently, you have no memory of our bringing you home."

"No." My voice dropped to a shamed whisper. "I don't."

Later, my father came over and joined Mom and me in the living room.

"Do you realize what you're doing to yourself?" he asked.

I picked at my jeans.

"Look at you. You're a skeleton. What are you taking? What are you drinking?"

Shock electrified through me. Never had either parent ever verbally discussed any issue of the home, and especially nothing unpleasant. Even when my mother found my scale, she merely removed it. She never challenged my actions.

"Don't you realize I buried three family members in one year?" Dad's voice rose. "They *all* died because of alcohol."

His voice caught, and he wiped tears from his eyes.

"I don't want to lose you, too."

I dropped my head. *How could I hurt Dad so bad?*

"I promise I'll straighten out. I'll start by going to AA."

ॐॐॐ

AA changed my life, but not in the usual way. I met Rocky, a fellow attendee and bad guy trying to beat jail time through their inpatient program for heroin addiction.

An attraction was planted, grew and bloomed — all at my first meeting.

Rocky moved on to a halfway house where I was allowed to visit, so I brought him cookies. Next, he moved in with his mother, and I moved in with him. The challenge to fix him while so broken myself appealed to me. His attraction to me was his need for a "sugar mama."

I loved taking care of him and loved his need of me. I thrived on the chaos of his life, even while his continuing heroin habit drained me of my paychecks. My body wore out from our high-tension lifestyle.

Two years into the relationship, I realized I was pregnant.

Something's got to change. I passed a hand over my flat belly. *I have a real life growing in here. A little helpless life that's going to need tending and protection.*

When Rocky went off to jail again, I decided to enroll in the local university. I delivered our daughter Zoe and earned a degree in elementary education.

I got a job, an apartment and a car. I'd socked away $8,000 by the time Rocky got out of jail. I anticipated a new season of rescuing my prince, but I learned he'd picked up a new girlfriend.

Anxious to keep him, I started using heroin with him. We snorted away my savings account, injected heroin and got ejected from my apartment. I lost my job. Lastly, I lost my car.

Rocky returned to jail, and I checked myself into a 45-day rehab program. After completing the course, I got a job waitressing, found an apartment for Zoe and me and began living as a responsible adult.

"I want to see you, babe." Rocky called just before his release.

"I'm done. Leave me alone."

"Where are you staying now?"

"I'm not saying. I'm through with you."

A few weeks later, I answered a knock on the door. Rocky stood there grinning.

"How did you find me?" I gasped.

"Does it matter?" His grin widened.

I let him in, and again, my finances drained out as we both returned to using heroin.

༷ ༷ ༷

A year later, I drove to the preschool to pick up Zoe.

"She's not here," her teacher said.

"What?" My voice rose to a shriek. "Where is she? What happened?"

"You'll have to check with the principal. I don't know where she is."

I raced to her office. "Where's my daughter?" I demanded.

"I'm sorry."

You don't look sorry.

"Your father came here along with the sheriff." Her eyes flicked over my gaunt frame. "I had no choice but to release Zoe into his custody."

I stormed back to my car and drove home, furious. Another sheriff waited by the curb and served me with official papers.

I called Mom's number. No answer. I called Dad. Again, no answer. I called Dylan. Same result.

"I'll show you!" I screamed in the empty apartment. I shot more heroin than before. Six months later, my fury abated, my resources dried up and I hit bottom.

"Mom."

"Pearl! How are you? Where are you?"

"Mom," I choked. "Can I come home?"

"Of course."

I arrived at her door, penniless. Track marks snaked up my arms, and bruises polka-dotted my skin. My too-short hair smelled, and I reeked of hopelessness.

"What have you done to yourself?" Anger and concern clouded her eyes. "Come in here, and get cleaned up."

I spent the next year parked on Mom's couch, drinking wine and listening to the radio. I had little interest in life or recovery. *I've lost everything, and for what? Even Zoe. Dylan has her. How he resented watching me as a child and being the father figure when Dad was gone, and now he's watching my child. I have nothing left to lose. My life is over.*

I was 30.

ॐ ॐ ॐ

Orin

I forged my identity in prison but longed for a real life on the outside. I wanted a wife, kids and home. I fathered a son and a daughter during two of those brief periods of freedom but parented neither, because the overwhelming desire for a single drink led to another and then back to drug use — which sent me back to jail. I wanted to help my son with Little League and coach him in Pee Wee football, but heroin blocked the way. Instead, my children heard empty promises from a desperate father unable to fulfill a single one because of the consequences of a habit he couldn't break. The next quarter century passed in a blur of highs, lows, theft, jail, prison, drinking and homelessness.

In prison, I became somebody. My many returns honed my senses, and like Red explained about Brooks' suicide in the movie *Shawshank Redemption*, I became institutionalized. I wanted to be on the outside but couldn't make it on the outside. Within four months of release, I'd be back because the need for heroin ate up every penny earned or stolen.

People tired of me, and eventually nobody offered me a place to crash or a couch to rest on. I stayed in the shed of a quasi-friend after one release. It was the day after Christmas. I was 37 with no reason to celebrate the season. I dealt and used from his hovel. During a drug deal gone bad, a guy snuck up behind me and slugged me in the head with a baseball bat.

More focused on my next fix, I had no interest in having a doctor check out the injury. Worn out by life and drugs, I crawled into the shed where I'd been staying and fell asleep. When I awakened the next day, I found myself lying in my own feces.

"You need to see a doctor," a friend advised.

"No. Go get some heroin. I'll be fine."

Is this all there is to life? Living from fix to fix? Lying in my own mess? I longed for death to free me. I looked like a zombie and felt twice as dead.

છેન્છેન્છે

Pearl

It took a year for my exhausted body to recover from the abuse of meth and heroin. As strength crept back, I remembered some guy friends from high school and gave them a call.

"George, I need help. Real help. Can I come to church with you?"

"Of course! Where do you live now? We'll come get you this Sunday."

I had attended church with George, his mother and brother Jason when I was pregnant with Zoe. I felt that only God, if there was a God, could help me now.

"We go to a Bible study on Tuesday nights," George said when he picked me up. "Would you like to come to that, too?"

"I need something. I'll come."

"Good. We're studying *The Purpose Driven Life*. Have you ever heard of it?"

"No."

"It was written by Rick Warren. He says that every human, at one time or another in life, will ask themselves, 'Why am I here?' He maintains that we are *all* here for a reason — a purpose — and by seeking God, we can learn it."

"My life has absolutely none." I struggled to keep bitterness from my voice. "I haven't seen my daughter for two years because my parents decided I was an unfit mother. They had the sheriff kidnap her and give her to my brother."

"Have you ever heard of Get Real Ministries?" a lady at the Bible study asked.

"No, I haven't."

"You should check it out. The New Hope International

Church off Highway 242 in Concord hosts it. Get Real reaches out to people on the streets and helps them become productive in society again."

"Sounds like something I need."

About 75 people gathered the first time I attended Get Real. We sang wonderful songs about God's love and power for 45 minutes before Pastor Willy got up to speak.

"You may not have any hope for yourselves, but I'm here to tell you that God still works miracles today. He still raises the dead. I was dead in alcohol, but now I've been sober for 12 years. Not on Willy's strength, but with God's. Only God can defeat Satan's plan of destruction for your life. God has *good* plans for your life, according to Jeremiah, chapter 29. Plans for you to prosper and succeed."

A sliver of hope flickered in my heart while I listened to Pastor Willy talk. *I have to stay plugged in to these people.*

I continued going to George's church after starting the Get Real program at NHIC but felt conflicted. *I need to be faithful to one church. I like George's church, but if I'm going to Get Real at NHIC, maybe I should go to that church.*

During my first visit at NHIC, the musicians began singing, "I'm forgiven because you were forsaken. I'm accepted, you were condemned …"

The worship music continued flowing over me and penetrated my empty, dead heart.

They sang a song by Chris Tomlin with the words,

"Amazing love, how can it be/that you, my God, should die for me."

Tears watered the cold, hard ground. *God, I'm so sorry for turning my back on you. I accepted Jesus as my Savior back in George's church when I was pregnant, but I never yielded to him as Lord. I want to do that now because I know if I don't, I will self-destruct forever. I miss my dad. I miss my daughter. Will you take over and be the king of my life as that song says?*

"I've called your brother," Mom said to me the following month. "I told him how much you've changed, and I believe it's real this time. We're ready to consider giving Zoe back to you."

"Mommy!"

"Zoe!" My daughter rushed into my waiting arms. We'd not seen one another for more than two years. We clung to each other and cried. *Thank you, God. Thank you for this miracle.* I twirled my daughter around in my arms, and we cried some more.

My heart and body continued to heal, but I longed for the day God would heal the relationship between my father and me. My endless lies had driven him from me.

"Hi, Dad." I was surprised when six months after Zoe's return he walked into the diner where I waitressed the midnight shift. He sat down in my section.

"Your mother tells me you've changed."

I slid in the bench across from him.

"Yes, I have, Dad. Or rather, God changed me, because I certainly couldn't do it on my own."

His eyes grew moist. "I would like to believe you."

"You don't have to try, Dad. Just let God show you how much *he* has changed me. Have you ever heard of *The Purpose Driven Life*?"

He shook his head.

"Well, God has shown me that I *do* have purpose here on earth. I have value. He took me from being a wasted junkie to where I am now. I'm working. I have an apartment, and I have Zoe back. Most importantly, I have a real, living, vital relationship with Jesus."

He nodded. "I'd like to hear more."

"I'll be happy to tell you more."

∾∾∾

Orin

Not long after the baseball bat bashing incident, I found a way to return to prison — the only place I felt at home and understood the way things ran.

After more than 20 years of experience, I became the older, more-experienced guy who young punks either looked up to or feared.

One Sunday morning, I noticed other inmates filing back to their units after chapel, each with a Bible tucked under one arm. *Suckers. Always hiding behind some yahoo religion.*

Suddenly a yearning hit me. *They all look like they haven't a care in the world.* I wondered how inmates could have such calm faces.

What do I have to lose? Oh, yes, my dignity. Well, there wasn't anything dignified about sleeping in my own waste. Maybe I need to check it out. One time can't hurt.

The following Sunday, when call for chapel blared over the intercom, I stepped into the hallway. I glanced over my shoulder. *I hope I don't see anyone I know. It would ruin my reputation if anyone saw me as weak.* I shuffled in and parked in a rear seat.

"God demonstrates his own love for us in this: While we were still sinners, Christ died for us" (Romans 5:8). The man at the pulpit read from his well-worn Bible.

"Guys, we are all sinners. *All* of us. Some of you have chosen wild sins, such as drinking or drugs or even murder. Others choose more subtle sins. Gossip. A little embezzlement. Fudging books.

"Sin is sin. And Jesus died for *all* sin. His cousin John pointed out Jesus to his own followers and said, 'Look, the Lamb of God, who takes away the sin of the world' (John 1:29). There is no list of which sins are white, black, gray or otherwise. Jesus paid for *all* the sins of the world.

"So, no matter what you've done, no matter what got you into this place, God wants you to know that he sent Jesus to die on the cross to take care of it. Can you, will you, accept his offer of forgiveness and grace?"

I mulled over the message after I got back to my cell. Someone had handed me a used Bible. I sat on my bunk and talked to this unknown God, trying to wrap my head around the idea that he could and would freely forgive my decades of failure and filth.

"If you're real," I prayed deep within me, "and you really will forgive me, you'll have to prove it." I took my new/used Bible and opened it. I stared at the words highlighted in unmanly bright pink: "'Come now, let us settle the matter,' says the Lord. 'Though your sins are like scarlet, they shall be as white as snow; though they are red as crimson, they shall be like wool'" (Isaiah 1:18).

My mouth dropped open. *Is this for real? God wrote those words — who knows how long ago — and I'm reading them now? "Even if your sins are like scarlet." I guess that means the worst of the worst. I ain't done murder, but my sins are bad enough. And God wants to negotiate with me?*

I thought back to the message I'd heard at chapel. According to the speaker, God wanted to swap my sinful, weary, lifeless heart for a pure one that beat in his forgiving love. I chewed on the idea, trying to make sense of it. Idly my hands flipped a few pages.

"Come, all you who are thirsty, come to the waters; and you who have no money, come, buy and eat ... Why spend money on what is not bread, and your labor on what does not satisfy? Listen, listen to me, and eat what is good ... hear me that your soul may live ... Seek the Lord while he may be found; call on him while he is near. Let the wicked forsake his way and the evil man his thoughts. Let him turn to the Lord, and he will have mercy on him … 'For my thoughts are not your thoughts, neither are your ways my ways,' declares the Lord. 'As the heavens are higher than the earth, so are my ways higher than your ways and my thoughts than your thoughts … You will go out in joy and be led forth in peace.'"

I stared out at the square of blue sky available to me. *You would do this for me, God? You would wipe away 40 years of crap — just like that?*

Just like that.

You really mean it?

Try me and see, God seemed to say, again deep within my spirit.

If you're willing to forgive me of all my stupidity and sin, then the least I can do is give you all my life.

I'll take it.

A few days later, one of the home boys approached me. "Hey, Orin," he said, slapping me on the back. "Can I get you to pray for my mom? I got a letter today and found out she's really sick."

"Me? Why do you want *me* to pray?"

"Don't know." He stopped to study me. "You're different. Don't know what's going on with you, but you've changed. It shows in your face."

Other inmates began approaching me with prayer requests, so I started a prayer group and even a Bible study on our cell block.

Understanding traveled at Mach speed for this new kingdom — God's kingdom — I found myself in, a welcome change from speeding down the old route of death and destruction.

⥁⥁⥁

You need to check this place out, my good friend wrote. *This is a long-term treatment center for drug and substance abuse. See if you can get the judge to release you to come here. I'll be waiting to greet you when you come!*

I tucked the letter in my Bible. *This is ridiculous,* I thought, *actually, it's impossible. Completely impossible. I'm in for a long stretch. There's no way a judge will release me anywhere with my record.*

Ask. You'll never know if you don't.

By that time, I was used to hearing God talking in my heart. Even so, doubt remained. "It would take a miracle to go."

When did I run out of power? God seemed to ask.

I contacted my lawyer who did the necessary research and presented my case before a judge. I stood before her — speechless. My mind still refused to process the reality, even on the drive to the rehab center.

"Good evening." I watched the speaker on my first night there. "I am Willy Vega. God delivered me from alcohol abuse, and now I lead Get Real Ministries at New Hope International Church. Get Real reaches out to recovering addicts with weekly celebrations and other means of support. I can only do this through God's power, for I have none."

"Would you be interested in coming to Get Real at NHIC to give testimony on how much God has changed you?" Pastor Willy asked me a few weeks later.

"I'd be so honored," I said.

I moved on to a halfway house and continued my involvement at Get Real and attendance at NHIC.

"Would you like to come to my house?" a member of NHIC asked me. "A few men get together, and we study the Bible and how it relates to our everyday lives."

I hesitated. The only place I'd ever felt completely at home was in prison where I ruled as Mr. O, the inmate no one ever messed with.

"I'll come."

I gathered with the other men. Men in touch with God, themselves and their families. At first I felt awkward, but gradually their unconditional acceptance and love eased my apprehensions. I sensed the brotherhood they shared, stronger and truer than any I'd known in prison or on the streets.

God, this is where I want to be. I want to surround myself with people like this — men and women with integrity. I want to walk with you in the same confidence I see in them.

I longed for a real marriage partner as so many of my new church friends had. *God, if it's okay with you, could you send me a woman who could love me? She has to love you more than she'd ever love me. And, if it's okay, could you make her easy on the eyes?*

❧❧❧

Two years into recovery, I spotted an attractive woman named Pearl attending a Get Real celebration. She sat all hunched over and withdrawn until the music began. Then she seemed to unfold and grow like a thirsty flower drinking up water.

I watched her progress from hopelessness to a woman of deep faith in God for two more years before asking for a date.

"Would you like to have coffee with me?"

"Um, no, thank you. I don't know you, and I'm not interested in any relationships at the moment."

"That's okay." Inside, I breathed a bit of relief, but as time went on, deep down, I felt God had set Pearl aside for me.

I continued working and helping at Get Real Ministries and the church. I prayed God would bless Pearl and her daughter Zoe with health and happiness. Pearl remained friendly but aloof.

"Drop everything and meet us at Yogurt World." I read the text from Zoe with amazement and confusion, but I obeyed — pronto. After another two years of waiting, my heart beat with hopeful anticipation.

Pearl and Zoe waited for me. I sat across from both, and we began to talk. And talk. Common history and victories meshed our hearts together.

We married four months later. I gazed into the eyes of

my lovely bride, my gem, my Pearl, and my heart swelled with love and gratitude.

❧❧❧

"Come get this baby before I bash its head against a wall," the frantic mother cried over the phone.

"Change of plans," I told Pearl. "We have to go pick up a baby — right now."

We became actively involved in a ministry through NHIC called Safe Families for Children. We opened our home as a pre-foster care refuge on the behalf of parents in crisis before they lose their children to the foster care system. Our goal is to strengthen families, not divide them.

"How things have changed," she observed as we raced toward the address given. "Not that many years ago, *my* daughter was rescued from *me*. I know how it felt to love her so much and yet to know that I was totally unfit to care for her."

"As was I. All my life I sought a dad and let the older men in prison become my father figures. Then heroin kept *me* from being the father I should have been to my own two children."

"Isn't it just like God to take our biggest failures and turn them into blessings? Now, we can reach out and help other 'unfit' parents by temporarily keeping their children until they get their own lives together."

"And, not only that, but he gave us two more children

of our own to raise right. Like a second chance at parenting."

"Let's pray before we go to the door," Pearl said as I parked the car in front of the caller's house.

"Good idea. God, be with us and with this family. Please help us protect this baby until these parents have clear minds. Help this mom and dad make good choices, and give them the power to be transformed. Lord, please change their lives as radically as you did ours. In Jesus' name, amen!"

TRANSFORMED
The Story of Adam
Written by Ameerah Collins

My whole life I've felt different. Is this where I belong?
The thought muddled my mind even more than the eerie environment I'd stumbled upon. I coughed and waved a puff of smoke from my face. Music pounded as bodies twirled across the dance floor. I eyed the line at the bar. Men, dressed as glitzy women, talked and laughed with one another. They had such exaggerated feminine mannerisms, though. Their faces were thick with makeup, and their voices held a certain inflection.

They're all men, but they're dressed up like women. Maybe this is how I should be. Am I gay? Am I straight? I don't know. I'm so confused.
Cheers and screams suddenly echoed in the air. A rainbow of lights flickered across a platform on one side of the room. Men in glimmering gowns and big hair strutted onto the stage. They performed as drag queens, dancing and singing as they engaged the crowd so easily. They gestured to members of the audience, singling out guys and causing a thrilling sensation to rumble throughout the place. Transfixed, my eyes followed one transsexual. She was strikingly beautiful. I was instantly drawn to her. She didn't seem fake. She looked like an actual woman.

She's a woman trapped in a man's body, but she's bringing the female in her out. That's what I am! I'm like

139

her. I want to look like her. I want to be like her. I need to do something about it.

I continued to admire the performers from afar. The strategically painted lines on their faces, the proud self-acceptance they portrayed, the fabulous vibes they oozed so naturally. I wanted to climb onstage with them. I wanted to escape my life as a confused man and immerse myself in the world of drag.

No, no, I can't do that. What will people think? What will my family say?

No one knew of my identity crisis. It was my own little secret — a secret that needed to remain hidden.

I don't know how I'm going to achieve looking like these girls, but one day I will.

I promised myself: One day, I'd be a woman.

રે રે રે

Ever since I was 5 years old, I knew I was different. I didn't experience any dramatic childhood trauma or suffer through any sort of abuse. I just didn't fit in. I was raised in a Christian home with my two sisters, Sherri and Terri, and two brothers, David and Albert. My parents kept us in church, and my mother ingrained the importance of prayer and God into our lives at an early age. Still, having such a big family and living in a loving home didn't make me feel any less alone.

Growing up, I constantly compared myself to my brothers and the other neighborhood boys. They just had this natural roughness and boyish behavior that I never seemed to develop. They played outdoor games that I just wasn't into. I tried my hardest to be like them, but no matter how much I forced myself to act like them, grownups could see through my pretense.

"What's up with Adam? He always shies away when the boys get too rough," one neighbor asked my mother. I stood in a corner, listening to them talk around the kitchen table.

"He just doesn't like to get dirty. He's a little different. So what?" Mom replied.

"He's shy," a cousin added. "Why is he so timid? The boy's afraid of his own shadow."

"No, just shy. But he'll grow out of it."

I should have been born like my sisters. That idea stuck in my mind. I repeatedly wondered, *Why am I boy? I want to be like Sherri and Terri. I wish I was born a girl.*

As I eavesdropped on adults talk about my behavior, I realized I needed to keep my feelings to myself. If they already didn't believe I was like the other boys, even though I really tried to be, they'd *really* talk about me if they knew I wanted to be like my sisters.

So, throughout grade school, I bottled up my secret and ensured no one found out about it. I didn't tell my brothers or sisters what was going on with me, but part of me knew they deemed me a little peculiar. They didn't treat me any differently for my oddness, though. My brothers still involved me in their lives, and my sisters loved me the same. My siblings never really mentioned my oddness or reclusiveness. They just let it be.

In high school, I began to feel even more out of place. I went to a predominantly white school with only a few black people. Not only did kids look at me as if I didn't belong because I was one of the few blacks there, but I still struggled with my sexuality. I found it hard to make friends with the other students. I didn't want them to find out I was uncomfortable in my own skin, so I just steered away from everyone.

During lunchtime, I helped the cafeteria workers so I'd have an excuse not to mingle with my peers. I ended up making one friend, though. Ivan knew I was different than the other guys there, but he befriended me, anyway. He didn't judge me for not fitting in with his friends, and he didn't shun me when I became a bit more comfortable around him and my oddities began to show even more. Although Ivan was my friend, I never talked to him about my conflicted boy/girl feelings. I kept it inside, afraid to truly accept what I was feeling.

When I graduated from high school, I'd already joined the Job Corps. I was eager to move into the student dorms, where I wouldn't have to worry about my family looking at me all the time and overhearing people talk about me. I just wanted to break free.

I also wanted to figure out if I was gay, straight or what. The uncertainty still confused me. I didn't feel like a guy. I felt like I should have been born a girl. *But does that make me gay? If I think I'm a girl, wouldn't that mean I'm actually straight?*

One night, I went out and found myself in a gay

nightclub. I had no idea how I ended up there; it was almost as if something led me there. I didn't even realize it was a gay environment until I noticed many of the men were flashy, flamboyant and very feminine. I became transfixed as I gazed around the room. I took in every little piece of what I saw.

Transsexuals, drag performances, beautiful women who were actually men — I just couldn't believe what I was seeing. My heart pounded as I admired one particular transsexual. She seemed so confident, as if she would have dared anyone to tell her she wasn't a woman. Her body looked so feminine, like she'd been born with a busty chest and delicate features. *I want to be her,* I told myself. *I need to be her. This is what I've been missing. This is what I've been feeling. I'm a woman stuck in a man's body. Just like these people here.*

I didn't exactly know how I would achieve it, but I made a vow that one day I'd become just like those drags. I thought of how my family would respond to the transformation I'd make someday. *Would their Christian values help them to accept me or cause them to reject me?* I wondered. But in that moment, all I could do was stare.

Stare and trust that I'd be just like those transsexuals — one day.

☙☙☙

As I continued in my Job Corps education program, I didn't tell anyone about my venture into the gay nightclub. I was still confused about my sexual identity; I had yet to define myself as a female or male. I was so unsure. When I went home to see my family, I acted like the boy my mother gave birth to. The Adam she knew and loved. However, my heart was someplace else. It was still in that nightclub with all those drags.

Later, my school assigned me a gay roommate. Shane was a loud, attention-seeking sort of guy. He always told stories about his oh-so-glamorous life, what he did this night or that night, how he went to this place and that place. Shane was just an interesting character to sit back and listen to. Over time, he seemed to make up his mind about my sexual orientation. He noticed my lack of manliness. He had it in his stubborn head that I was gay and just didn't know it. He flirted with me, made moves on me and tried to test me once.

"Oh, c'mon, Adam! You know you're different than other guys here. I like you." He grinned slyly. "Don't you like me, too?"

"Sure, Shane, but not in a romantic way. I don't like you like that." I backed away from him as he edged closer to me. I bumped into the bathroom door and planted myself against it.

"What do you mean, *like that?*" His eyes crossed in irritation, as if I'd offended him. "You're gay, aren't you? You're just like me. I know you are. All the gay boys love me!"

"What?" I said, my voice heightening. "I never said I was gay! I don't know what I am. I'm trying to figure it out. But I do know I just like you as a friend. I'm not looking for anything more."

Shane grabbed my arm, jerked me toward him. I immediately pushed him away. I scrambled into the bathroom, slammed the door and locked it behind me. Shane banged on the door. I pressed my body against it, breathing hard. He taunted me, and I shuddered at his words. I stayed in the bathroom for an hour, waiting for Shane to back off and accept I didn't want him as a boyfriend, only a friend. After that traumatizing event, Shane left me alone about my sexual orientation confusion, but his behavior that day scared me. I couldn't believe he'd reacted to my rejection in such a crazy way.

The next time someone tested me happened after our school scheduled construction for my side of the dormitory, and Shane and I were given temporary housing. I was assigned to bunk for the night with Peter, a fellow student. Before bed, I went out with a few of my friends. We walked around Hollywood, just hanging out. We met some older guys, went back to their house and partied.

I got completely drunk and could barely function. I didn't realize how much of a lightweight I was, I just drank what the guys offered me. They tried to make out with us. The rum and the heat from the hot tub coupled with my own confusion and constant internal turmoil caused me to be sickened by their advances. All the flirting was just getting on my nerves, so we decided to return to campus.

When I stumbled to my assigned room for the night, I became even more disgusted. Peter had pushed the beds together, making a big bed.

"What is this?" I screeched. I clutched my head, still feeling dizzy from the alcohol. Peter lay on the mattresses — like he was waiting on a specific someone.

"Where have you been?" he asked with a raised brow.

"We went to Hollywood tonight and partied," I said distractedly.

I ran to the bathroom, burst through the door and puked in the toilet. I shook my head as I flushed, staring into swirling chunks I'd consumed just hours before. I hobbled out of the bathroom.

"Why are the beds pushed together? Don't you have a girlfriend?"

Why would he push the beds together? Peter and his girlfriend are always hugging on campus. Everyone sees them. Is he gay? He can't be gay? What would his girlfriend think?

"Just chill, man." Peter propped his chin on his elbows as if the whole situation was just normal. "Don't read too much into it."

I don't know what to do. How am I supposed to react to this? This is so weird.

Drunk and vulnerable, I threw caution to the wind and crawled in the bed with Peter, trying to process how I could be sharing a bed with this seemingly straight guy.

More confused than ever, I thought about how Peter could do that to his girlfriend.

How could he hide his sexual preference so easily?

One supposedly straight guy. One majorly confused guy.

In the same bed. Together. Like it's nothing.

What in the world was I thinking?

ళళళ

In my early 20s, I worked at an architectural firm. I still harbored a secret desire to be like the transsexuals from the nightclub I'd visited years before, but I had yet to take a step toward transforming myself into a female. I still viewed myself as a woman trapped in a man's body, but I was just scared to pursue it.

One year, the company I worked for decided to host a talent show for all the employees. It simply served as a sort of team building function for everyone to mingle together. When I first heard about the talent show, I instantly pictured the drag performances. I believed I could use the talent show as a way to live out my fantasy of being a drag.

I'd always concealed the real me at work, school and with my family. So I used the talent show to display myself to the world, or rather my co-workers, but it felt like I was opening myself up to the world. I wore high heels, dusted my face with makeup, danced and lip-synced to music. I worked the crowd just like the drag queens did, and I felt amazing.

I feel so secure in this identity, I told myself. *I belong. I want to do this professionally.*

So I did.

For years, I worked in drag nightclubs. I became so obsessed with the drag life — it became my sole focus. It was my escape from my normal life and its limitations. Nearly every night, I lived out my fantasy as a woman. It was like I wore one mask during the day, and I wore another mask of pure drag at nightfall. I kept it a secret for a few years, but in my late 20s, I decided to share the most private part of my life with my family.

"I'm not going to lie, Adam. I don't like it." Sherri, my older sister, crossed her arms and shook her head at me. "It just — it seems pretty sick. I can't accept this."

"It's not *sick*, Sherri," I softly said. "I feel at home when I'm in drag. I belong."

"Okay. Wrong word." She sighed and glanced at my silent mother. "But it *is* unnatural."

"I can't help it that I feel this way. It's no secret I've always been, well, odd."

"I don't like this, either, Adam." My mother's gentle voice spoke up. "I'll love you. I'll pray for you to change. You're my son. But just know that I do not accept this drag life."

My other sister and two brothers said they loved me. They didn't express their feelings about my drag involvement, but they didn't openly criticize it, either. They just loved me.

As I continued to do my drag performances, I plunged so deep into the lifestyle that I began thinking God made a mistake with me. I was 28 years old, and my feelings of wishing I'd been born a female reached a new level. So I went to see a doctor who specialized in hormone replacement therapy. The doctor and I had extensive conversations about my sexual identity and how I perceived myself as a person. It was all part of the requirements prior to receiving hormone replacement therapy. I talked to some of my transsexual friends about it, too.

"I went to see a doctor about hormone replacement therapy," I told my friend Brody. He sat beside me at the bar. "He already started me on the estrogen pills. I'll get the shots soon."

"Whoa! Seriously?" Brody laughed with glee. "That's great, Adam! I should have told you sooner, but I went to see a doctor, too."

"Really? Why didn't you tell me?"

"Well, why didn't *you* tell *me*?" He chuckled and stirred his cocktail. "I don't know. It's just something I needed to keep to myself for a while. Ya know?"

"Yeah, me, too." I nodded. "I understand. I'm going to let my bosses at the architecture firm know what's up. I don't want to surprise them when my body starts changing."

"Right, right. Good idea."

"I want to change my name, too." I shrugged. I was still hesitant about letting someone in on all my thoughts. "I won't be Adam anymore. I'll be Andrea."

He playfully nudged my shoulder. "Looks like we're going through this together, huh?"

"I don't feel so alone with the change now that I know you're going through it, too."

I told my bosses about my plans to become a woman. They changed all my personal data at work and helped me complete the necessary paperwork to change my name to Andrea. Suddenly, it all became so real.

Steadily, my chest began to grow. The female characteristics I'd always dreamed of having were finally forming. I got the hormone shot every two weeks. Each shot the doctor gave me just encouraged me to maintain my femininity — to continue acting, being and believing I was the dainty and beautiful woman I wanted to be. The hormone therapy thinned and smoothed my skin, my hair grew longer and I needed to shave less frequently. Each time a little strand of facial hair grew, I quickly plucked it out. The changes just felt so natural. At least I wanted to believe they were natural.

તે તે તે

In my 30s and early 40s, I regarded myself as a full-fledged woman. I wanted to have reassignment surgery to complete the physical transformation, but each time I signed up for a surgery, it never went through. That really annoyed me. I ended up becoming involved with a guy named Bo. He seemed pleasant when I first met him. He was a headstrong guy and liked to cook. After dating for a while, we moved in together. I began to notice his ill treatment of others, and that worried me.

One day, he's going to treat me like that. He'll turn on me. He won't be Mr. Nice Guy anymore.

It was a distressing thought that lingered in the back of my mind. I knew he had a mean streak, and he struggled with abandonment issues from some sort of childhood trauma. It was just a matter of time, I figured, before he took his pain out on me.

Deep in the relationship and still doing drag performances, I began doing drugs. I smoked marijuana and other drugs to take the edge off. Bo cursed. We fought. He usually had the upper hand because he was bigger than me. Our relationship was always up and down. One day he would come home as the nicest man on earth, the next day he'd raise all sorts of drama. I hated it, but I couldn't blame everything on him. I had my own problems. My drug use had become an addiction, and I stayed high. I always threatened to leave him because of his cruel ways, and he always flew off the handle when I did.

"You're going to walk out on me, aren't you?" Bo shouted at me in the living room of our apartment. He pushed me and poked his finger in my chest.

"What are you talking about?" I rolled my eyes and puffed on a blunt.

"Don't screw with me, Andrea! You want to leave me. I know you do. You're just like the rest of them!" He threw his fist into the wall beside my head, and I flinched.

"Yeah, you're right!" I screamed right back at him. "I do want to leave you! You're always pushing me around and putting your hands on me. OF COURSE I WANT TO LEAVE!"

Bo snatched my arm and tossed me across the room. I stumbled onto the couch armrest, and when I whirled around, he backhanded me across my cheek. I screamed as the sting exploded across my face. I curled my fingers and punched him in his face. His head jerked to the side, and his breathing hitched. My throws always made him even more angry. He gripped my collar and hoisted me up against the wall, yelling obscenities in my face. I kicked and punched, but it didn't help. He always had the upper hand.

Every horrible clash ended with us making up. So many broken promises and hopeless apologies were thrown between us. They were all so false. They never *really* meant a thing. It was a vicious cycle that I just couldn't pull myself away from. Regardless of what Bo did, he kept me in his clutches, no matter what fiery words I spewed out.

As our relationship grew worse, my drug habit followed suit. I used the drugs to escape the reality of my life. I no longer received the satisfaction I once did from drag. I lost so much weight, and my time with Bo was ruining me. I didn't even recognize myself anymore.

Those weren't the only problems making me rethink my life choices, though. I had a terrible run-in with a man. I picked up a ride on the street once. I intended on doing a few things with him in his car, but he wanted to go to a hotel. The mention of a hotel instantly had me on guard. I didn't want to go. He was a bigger guy, pretty burly and obviously strong. If a fight broke out, he would get the better of me.

When we reached the hotel, I tightened my hold on my handbag, clinging to anything that I could. We entered a room, and he sprawled out on the bed. He wanted me to lie next to him.

"I don't want to do anything with you." I tried to be stern, but my nerves seeped out.

"C'mon." He harshly chuckled. "You've come all this way with me. You might as well just lie down with me. I won't hurt you."

I need to get out of here, I thought. *How am I going to get out of here?*

"Right." I inched toward the bed and placed my handbag on the nightstand. "I'll just lie next to you, but I'm not doing anything. I really, really don't feel comfortable doing anything."

He tucked his arm around me, and his hand flitted across my waist. I scooted away from him, but he kept coming closer. All of a sudden, he became forceful and aggressive. He flipped me on my back, and I slammed my hand against his chest to push him away. He didn't budge. He just loomed over me, pulling at my clothes and yanking at my skin.

"Get off of me!" I screamed and banged my arms against the wall above me. "NO! NO! I don't want to do anything! GET OFF! God, no! Don't let this happen to me. GOD, HELP!"

"Stop yelling!" he shouted, his searing-hot breath in my ear. "You're mine! You came here with me. You're mine tonight."

God, please save me, I begged in my mind. *I don't want to be here. I shouldn't have got in his car. Please, God, please save me. I need you to save me.*

With a great force, I pressed my hands against the man's chest and pushed him off me. He flew back and landed on the ground. I jumped from the bed, grabbed my handbag and ran to the door. He beat me there. His large body stood in front of it, panting.

"It's too late, now," he yelled with his fist tightened at his side. "YOU'RE MINE!"

He dove toward me to tackle me. I swiftly leapt off to the side, and he missed me. I ran toward the door with my bag in tow. I heaved the door open and sped down the hall to the exit. My heart pounded as I ran and ran until I was far from the hotel.

Never in my life had I been so afraid. I firmly believed I'd made it out of there only because of God, because I'd called out to him for help. I'd screamed, yelled and banged against the walls, but no one in the hotel came to help me — but God did. There was no way I should have been able to push that big man off of me. How did he miss me when he tried to tackle me? *It was all God,* I decided. Even though I was living such a shabby life, God came to my rescue. He saved me, and that made me think of him more. I'd always considered myself a Christian because of the way I was raised. I knew I believed in God, but I also knew I wasn't living the way the Bible said Christians should live.

How could God love me enough to save me, when I was so disobedient?

Not long after, I broke up with Bo. I told him I couldn't take it anymore, and we needed to end our relationship. I packed my bags, called my cousin very upset over the breakup and asked her to pick me up. Even though she felt my living choices and relationship with Bo were against God, she dropped everything and came for me. No questions asked. She just came.

When my cousin pulled up downstairs, I slowly descended the steps to her vehicle. I stopped at the last step and flopped down on it. Hesitancy filled my heart. I looked back to the top of the staircase and contemplated whether I really wanted to leave Bo. That's when I felt a nudge at my back. I looked behind me, but no one was there. Again, I thought of Bo. There was another push at my back, and I shook my head and stood with my bags.

"Okay, okay, I'm going." To anyone else, it looked as if I was talking to myself, but I believed I was talking to God and his angels. I believe he dispatched his angels to give me strength to leave that horrible situation. I felt his push at my back, as if a human being was physically touching me. *God wanted me to leave,* I realized. So I did.

When I loaded my things in the car and hopped in the passenger seat, my cousin smiled at me.

"Hey."

"Hi, cousin." I softly smiled but lowered my head. "Do

you think I can stay with you? Just for a little while? I need to get my life together, sort some things out."

"Of course, Adam — Andrea." Her hand grazed my shoulder. "Take as long as you need."

I stayed with my cousin for three months, and she helped me get off drugs. When I had withdrawal symptoms, she was there to see me through them. When I had cravings, she just prayed for me and stuck by my side. In those three months, I gained my weight back, restored my strength and put a hold on my drag life in order to detox and become healthy. I moved out into my own apartment and received an offer for a really good job. The location was great, the money was good and I had opportunities to advance.

While doing well in my new apartment and living clean, I learned that Bo wanted to move to my new apartment complex. Since we had to be neighbors, I said we could be friends but absolutely nothing more. Bo hated seeing me sober, at a healthy weight and happy without him.

One day he showed up in my apartment and beat me so badly that my neighbors ran to my apartment to help me. They called the cops and got Bo off me. After that, I could barely walk, and it took many months to return to normal. I was so over him this time. I knew for sure he was crazy, and I couldn't have him in my life.

☙ ☙ ☙

After cutting Bo off, I started really questioning my life. I'd thought about God often in the prior few years, but something was really gnawing at me. I just felt so damaged, broken and lost. My involvement with the drag life was over, but I kept taking my pills and shots for hormone therapy. I had no desire to get in any other romantic relationship. It seemed like I was steadily coming down from a rollercoaster I'd been on for so long. At first I enjoyed the ride, but it had just become tiring and even sickening to me.

I thought about all the situations I'd been in where I could have been seriously harmed or even killed, but whenever I called on God, he always saved me. *If I die today, will I go to heaven or hell?* I kept wondering this, but I couldn't determine the answer.

I just knew I wanted to get closer to God. I needed to know more about Jesus and gain a true understanding of the Christian life my mother raised me to pursue. Something prompted me to start studying the Bible and to turn on the TV to watch Christian programs on the inspirational networks.

I asked God questions within my heart, and I believe he led me to the answers in the Bible.

I came to a point where I ended up calling churches for prayer and Christian hotlines to talk about my life.

"I've been living a transsexual lifestyle for years now." I nestled the phone against my shoulder and propped open the Bible in my lap. "I've always felt like God made a mistake with me, ya know? Like I should have been born a female, instead of a male. And I guess my question is, if I die today, will I go to hell?"

"I'm going to tell you the truth," the man on the line said. "If you want to go to heaven, you need to make some serious changes in your life. I won't lie to you and tell you God is happy with the way you've been living. The truth is, he's been unsatisfied and hurt by your life choices for a long time now."

"Really?" I fingered the thin pages of my Bible as shame overwhelmed me. "I hurt God with my life?"

"Well, he cares for you. He loves you more than anyone on this earth ever can. If you want to live right by God, you have to give up the homosexuality, the transsexual life, everything has to go, my friend. You have to give it up."

"If I want more of Jesus, I have to give it up." I nodded, as tears slid down my face. "I want to give it all up. I want to give it up for God. How do I do that?"

"You ask for forgiveness, and you mean it. You turn away from your wrongdoing, and plant yourself in God's presence. You read the Bible, pray to him and ask for strength to live right. You got to cut it all off."

I decided to make my life right with God. I locked myself in my apartment for three months. I dropped to my knees and cried out to God. Never in my life had I ever cried so hard. The tears just overflowed, and I had no control over the shame, sorrow and remorse rolling through my entire body. I couldn't stop the deep need coiling within me, crying out to be saved.

"God, please forgive me for my sins." I sobbed with my head bowed. "I don't want to be a transsexual anymore. I don't want this life that is so against you, God. I don't want to be Andrea anymore, I want to be Adam again. I want my name back. Give me my name back, God, please!"

My body shook as the words tumbled off my tongue. "I want to be the man you made me to be. Take away the changes I've made in my body with all these chemicals. I know you're able, God. Please take it all away. Give me my masculinity back. I don't want to chase after men, I want to chase after you. I want to be who you created me to be."

I cried out to God for hours. I just completely opened my whole heart, mind and soul to him. I wanted him to fill me with his love. I felt like God listened to every word I said. I could feel him comforting me and filling my apartment with his massive presence. I felt he was there, and he was there for me. All the time, money and energy I put into transforming into a woman, I vowed to put that much effort into living right for God.

I rushed to my room, gathered up all my estrogen pills and flushed them down the toilet. I skipped every appointment I'd had scheduled with my doctor and never took another hormone shot again. In those three months, the only time I left the apartment was to go on grocery runs or pay bills. I only left if I truly needed to, and when I returned, I immersed myself in God. I prayed all day long. I constantly read my Bible. I talked to God about my innermost feelings and thoughts. I concentrated on God and handed my life over to Jesus Christ. All my time was devoted to getting closer to God and building a relationship with Jesus. I desired the Holy Spirit to live within me. The Bible taught me that God's Spirit would guide, comfort and help me. I needed God's power to live right. I needed his strength to battle my past.

I asked God to work on me throughout my lockup in my apartment. I believe he snatched away my desire for drag, men, drugs and anything that was unlike him. I believe he ripped all my wrong habits away and shoved them back to the pits of hell, exactly where I suppose they came from. Daily, I renewed my mind. I quoted scripture and reminded myself that I was a man of God. I was foolish to have wasted so many years living in darkness.

"The devil is a liar!" I shouted. "I'm not a woman stuck in a man's body. I am a man. I choose Christ. Devil, you've got to go!"

As I repeatedly spent time with God, and figuratively stomped on the devil's nasty head, God revealed so much to me. God knew I loved singing, but I felt like he told me I didn't have to use my talent in drag. I could use it to sing songs of love to him as a man of God.

I also came to recognize the many times God was there for me in my past, when I didn't even know it. I'd signed up for reassignment surgeries so many times, but they always fell through at the last minute. I came to believe it was God who wouldn't let me cross that line.

Each cancellation, I came to believe, was like God saying, *NO, ADAM! TOO FAR! NO!*

I even gathered all my makeup, female clothing, wigs and all the items I'd been collecting for so many years and gave them away to women I knew. The stuff they didn't want, I simply trashed. Then I called my brother.

"Hey, David." I held the phone to my ear and shuffled through my practically bare closet. "I really need some manly clothes. Can you help me out?"

"Uh, sure." David paused. "Are you all right? No one's seen you in a while. We've been worried. And, man, you sound — different."

"I'm great," I said, laughing. "I just need some clothes. I'll see you and the family soon."

My brother dropped off some clothes and shoes for me. I never wanted to look like a woman again. I started a rigorous exercise routine to rehabilitate my body and gain muscle. Steadily, my manly features returned. My chest flattened out, and my voice deepened. While I was taking the hormone therapy, a gap that I always had in my teeth bonded together for some reason. But I even credit God with giving me that small gap back. It was familiar, from when I still behaved as a man, and God allowed me to get it back. It was just something personal, and I believe he knew that.

After the three months ended, I came out of my apartment to see my family. They all huddled around me. They oohed and aahed at the sight of me. When I opened my mouth, they were shocked to hear my voice wasn't as feminine or high.

"Oh, my gosh!" Sherri covered her mouth with her

hands. She glanced at Terri, who looked at me with tears in her eyes. "What happened to you? You're so different!"

"Something good happened, sis. I got saved — I gave my life to Jesus!" I chuckled. "I'm done with everything. I'm over it all. God saved me."

David and Albert patted my back. "We knew you'd come back someday, bro."

"I got my name back, too. Legally." I smiled at my mother then. "I'm Adam again, Mom. Andrea is gone. I'm Adam."

"So many people have been praying for you for so long." Mom held back a light sob as she hugged me. "We've asked God to bring you back to him, and he did. He brought you back."

The following year, my neighbor Nina invited me to church one day. I was so surprised at her invitation, I asked if she was for real. I just couldn't believe I was good enough for church just yet. I was just a baby Christian — I had so much growing to do!

"Of course you can come to my church, Adam!" She laughed at my shocked expression. "Why wouldn't you be able to come?"

"I don't know. I just …" I sighed and scratched my head. "Are you sure?"

"Uh, yeah!" She grinned.

My first visit to New Hope International Church was so powerful. The message was everything I needed to hear. The pastor just seemed to touch on so much I'd dealt with my entire life. I believed his word was truly from the Lord.

Sitting in the pew and listening to the great songs to God, I couldn't help but get excited. I thought, *Oooh! I love this church!* The pastor even prayed with me after church and took time getting to know me.

I returned every Sunday after that. I attended Tuesday night Bible study. I signed up for classes on Wednesday to strengthen my knowledge and love for God. I just wanted to keep myself busy with the Lord. I didn't want to have any idle time on my hands and allow old thoughts to creep in. I just wanted my whole life consumed by God.

I grew close to the church members, and the brothers there welcomed me with open arms. They didn't judge me for my past or anything I may have been dealing with. They just encouraged me and helped me focus on God.

During my many activities at church, I ended up meeting Jamie. She didn't judge me, either. She became a close friend and confidante. Jamie was just so cool and fun.

We handed out church pamphlets in the community together and even worked in the church kitchen alongside one another. For some reason, we always ended up doing things together. And, eventually, we fell in love. I believe God placed us together. He gave me a woman who could love me for me and who I could love.

I remained mindful of my thoughts and actions. I believed the devil was slick and would try to get into my head and pull me away from God, so I worked to stay rooted in Jesus Christ. If I stayed wrapped up in God, I could overcome the enemy's advances. Sometimes I felt weak, and my confidence plummeted. But I'd say, "No. I am a strong man in Christ. Devil, you must flee!"

I once allowed emotions to rule my every action. I let them infiltrate my mind and make me believe things that I came to realize were totally untrue.

I once thought that homosexuality and transsexual living was just fine, because elements in society told me it was. I later realized that it was a lie and not from God. I no longer think people are born gay. I don't think that is true.

I believe God made me perfectly. I went through one transformation thinking God made a mistake. But when I decided to follow God, I underwent a new transformation. What I would call a *true* transformation — a transformed life through Jesus.

FROM NOTHING TO EVERYTHING
The Story of Stacey
Written by Laura Paulus

"Stacey, your grandma said you can't come to Thanksgiving dinner," my mom quietly told me.

My heart sank.

"It is just too hard on her to see you like this," she said. "She doesn't want you at the house at all."

My grandma, the one person I thought I could count on, does not even want to be around me? My heart ached. I felt betrayed. *How could I lose everything and everyone?* My dreams always included the house, the husband, the kids. Family mattered to me. I craved the American dream — the one that fulfills and makes you happy.

Instead, I had nothing.

Even being homeless would be easier to handle if I knew I was loved.

My first Thanksgiving without my husband and my kids was hard enough, thanks to the restraining order. I thought I still had some extended family supporting me, but no one seemed to want me around.

I told my boyfriend, Tony, "If my family wants me to get clean, then why are they treating me like this? I may as well be high since I have nothing to lose at this point."

"We can do whatever would help you feel better," Tony replied.

"Let's get some more drugs."

Tony, always willing to follow me anywhere, accepted my challenge. So that Thanksgiving day in 1994, we spent the holiday feasting on drugs.

It did not seem to matter how much we used, I couldn't numb the pain and anguish. Nothing could numb my heart enough.

Nothing.

And I realized that's all I had — nothing.

৵৵৵

Mom didn't drink back when I was born in 1964, but after growing up with an alcoholic stepfather, she was accustomed to the practice. The first chance she got to escape, she took it. That's when she married my dad. Dad learned about drinking from his parents. Even the family business supported my grandparents' favorite activity — my dad's parents owned a bar.

My parents married when my dad turned 21 and my mom was 16. They lived with my mom's mom after the wedding. My mom gave birth to me at the age of 17. Shortly after my arrival, my parents moved to their own place, but Grandma continued to be involved in our lives. My two sisters were born in quick succession after me.

We were always closer to my maternal grandmother, as we saw her more often. I have fond but fewer memories of my dad's parents. My favorite memories of Dad's mom include the pretty dresses and patent leather shoes she had ready for us to wear to church on the weekends we visited. She dressed us up and drove us over to the church.

Dad left us when I turned 5, and Mom raised us by herself with Grandma's help. By the time Dad abandoned us, he'd become a full-blown alcoholic. For several years, we had our little family of Mom and us girls. Then Mom married Larry, whom none of us kids really liked much. I never felt a deep connection with Larry or my mom, and my dad had left the picture. When I think back to those years, I remember feeling isolated most of the time.

Between my grandparents owning a bar and Mom and Larry always smoking marijuana around our house, it should be no surprise that I followed their example. At 13, I smoked pot for the first time. It became a regular habit, and I got caught enjoying some on my school campus after I turned 14. Before long, cigarettes and alcohol were a regular part of my life as well. I spent much of my time in high school partying with friends.

While much of my growing up years contain memories of drinking and smoking, something else stands out from that time. A bus from a local church came around to our neighborhood and picked up my sisters and me. For several years, we would attend services there every week.

Many memories from childhood revolve around the Sundays spent at that church. I fondly remember that the ladies not only taught us the books of the Bible, they gave us practical life lessons. We learned about how a lady should sit tall and straight and other important tips.

Mostly, I recall sitting and talking with them about anything and everything. The topic did not matter. Those ladies were really listening.

I mainly remember "Sister" Fudge and "Sister" Williams vividly. They were filled with such joy, and they smiled the whole time. They would lead all of the children in a time of singing together, and then they would separate us into groups by age and gender. We had room dividers to allow our time to be focused and private.

My time at this church was happy and filled with comfort. I could not wait to go every week. We laughed and played games, but we also learned about the Bible and other aspects of life.

❧❧❧

After graduating from high school in 1982, I moved in with my high school boyfriend on my 18th birthday. We lived together for a few years. Eventually that relationship crumbled, so I moved on with my life and secured my own place. I attended community college and worked. During this time, I began taking meth. In the beginning, it helped me feel less empty and broken inside. I enjoyed getting high.

A few years later, I met Brad. We lived together and then got married in May after I realized I was pregnant. A week before Christmas, our beautiful daughter arrived, and life changed. I had dreamed for so long of being a wife and mom, and finally I was both. I became thrilled when less than two years later, I gave birth to our son.

I dedicated myself to being a good wife and mom. I stopped the drugs. I did not need them now that I had my American dream of a home, marriage, little girl and little boy. At least that rang true for a while. I threw myself into caring for the children. They were my world.

Yet my heart felt tormented. No matter how much I tried, I could not be the type of mother I wanted to be. Marriage also turned out to be difficult. And in my misery, I sought out my old friend meth. Snorting meth was cheaper than drinking alcohol, and a neighbor gladly sold it to me.

Meth relieved my pain. It soothed my heart and the mom-guilt that lurked deep within. For a long time, I balanced things well enough that my drug habit remained controlled and hidden. But then the addiction started controlling me. I *needed* to get high. It became the most important thing to me, especially as my marriage deteriorated and I grew more overwhelmed.

❧❧❧

Brad and I separated in March 1994. We had reached a breaking point. The kids and I left and got our own place. Things steadily deteriorated. I grew desperate as the money dwindled. It would have been hard enough to make it financially as a single mom without addiction in the equation. I could not afford both housing and drugs, and we became homeless. As much as I wanted to make it work with my kids, I needed Brad to take them.

"Can you keep the kids while I find a place for us to live? I just need you to take them for a short time. I will get it all worked out," I assured him, while trying to convince myself.

"Are you still using?"

I had told Brad about the meth use when we were deciding to separate. Until then, I had been able to hide it. But he correctly realized I needed him to take the kids because of my drug addiction.

"Just take them for a few weeks to give me some time to get housing set up. Then we can resume our shared custody," I pleaded.

Then and always, Brad acted as a good dad and knew he needed to take our kids. I knew they would be well taken care of with him. What I did not know is that he would file to keep them. And I did not know that my own sister and mother would side with him and help him accuse me of being an unfit mother. Eventually, I came to see that they had to do it, but at the time, I felt my family betrayed me.

That September, the courts took custody of my children away from me. I missed so many precious moments with them: the first days of preschool, holidays, birthdays and many other moments.

I had lost a place to live.

I lost my children.

I lost *everything* to drugs and alcohol.

And I had nothing left but drugs and alcohol.

In November, the divorce became final — another

loss. And during that time, my mom and I discussed Thanksgiving dinner. Well, she discussed it. I attempted to comprehend what she was trying to tell me, that my grandma needed to protect her heart from watching me barely exist. I could not believe it. Grandma and I had always been close. I think part of it came from when my parents and I had lived with her my first months of life. And my sisters and I went and stayed with her many summers. I felt like she turned from me and betrayed me.

One support remained consistent — my friend Lori. She often talked with me on the phone and told me about God and how he cared about me.

Lori would pray for me. She encouraged me numerous times to enter a recovery program to rid my life of my addictions. I never thought that I needed it. I would have if I ever allowed myself to stop and think it through. This dear friend kept telling me that I needed to go and kept sharing a passage from the Bible that she knew I needed to hear. "If you declare with your mouth, 'Jesus is Lord,' and believe in your heart that God raised him from the dead, you will be saved" (Romans 10:9).

After my conversation with my mom regarding Thanksgiving, I realized that I had nothing else. I had literally lost everything. I had hit bottom, and I could not get any lower. I knew that Lori spoke the truth, and I needed to go to a recovery program.

On December 4, 1994, I entered a Christian recovery program. I vividly remember this date, because I not only began a new life as a recovering addict and alcoholic, I began a relationship with the Lord. There, at the bottom, I grasped how worthless my life had become. I realized that I'd failed and could not make sense of my life anymore. I certainly did not know how to fix it.

As the staff members spoke about God's love and healing power, I heard how my inner pain could be relieved. I learned of a way to feel loved and set free from my angst. I began to understand about how much Jesus loved me and how he had died for me. The words Lori shared with me just days before became real. I fully surrendered that day. I turned away from drugs and alcohol and turned to God.

Lori had also introduced me to my boyfriend, Tony, the August before I entered rehab. Tony and I hit it off instantly when we met, and we'd been inseparable. We brought out the worst in each other, from getting drunk to snorting and smoking methamphetamine. As long as we could party, we were up for whatever — until I went into treatment. I knew I had to do that on my own. And when he showed up to begin his own treatment a few days after I started, I told him that. I did not care how much he loved me. I needed to get my life figured out for me and for my kids who mattered most to me. Thankfully, Tony also chose to work on sobriety, and we were both able to finish the program.

I made some choices with Tony that I am not proud of, but they are also choices I would not change now. We were there to work on our addiction issues. However, given our weaknesses in every aspect of our lives, we became distracted. We complicated treatment with a continued sexual relationship. I became pregnant with my third child during my stay in the program. Nothing changed for me regarding my desire to stay off drugs and alcohol. In fact, it strengthened my resolve to leave the life of drugs far behind. And I had no problem telling Tony that leaving it all behind would be the only way he could remain a part of my life and our child's life. He did.

৵৵৵

After I completed the recovery program, I moved in with my mom and stepdad. I did this in order to find a job and save money until the baby arrived. I secured a job a month after moving in with them. I stayed with them for about five months. During that time, I worked and attended Bible studies and anything else I could at church. Church became the one place I truly felt at home, and I felt like I could not learn enough about God and his love for me.

I tried to share my new faith and the many things I had learned with my mom. She did not want to have much to do with it. She saw me going to AA meetings and could not grasp why, as she put it, I continued to hang out with addicts. But she also did not get why I wanted to hang out at church. She still supported me even if she did not understand it all. And when I moved out that August to live with Tony, we always came back for Sunday meals with my mom and stepdad. These allowed us to get closer to them, and I cherished those times.

My son entered the world that November, and Tony and I got married the next Valentine's Day in 1996. Marrying Tony remains one of the best decisions I ever made. And we adored our son from the moment he entered our lives.

However, my heart still ached to have my two older children with me. All along, authorities limited my visits with them to one hour every other Saturday. The visits were supervised the whole time.

I could not understand why I still could not have my children back with me after I had worked to change my life.

I spent many hours in prayer asking the Lord for the return of my children. Then one night as I struggled through the emotions of not having my children, I realized I needed to let it all go and trust that God would care for them. I cried out to God and told him, *I trust you to take care of these kids and protect them.* The next day, Brad called me and stated that the time had come to draw up new custody orders. We did and divided up visitation 50-50. Eventually, it became hard on my daughter to spend so much time apart from me. Her dad and I agreed to let her stay with me a majority of the time and visit him on the weekends. My son continued to split his time between us.

Brad and I went from hating each other and being enemies to working together for the good of our children. In fact, he had remarried, and when he and his wife were struggling to get pregnant, I prayed hard for them. Now they have three boys of their own. I believe that all of that is from God.

"Tony, can you believe the way that God moves?" I asked my husband. "He continues to be faithful to us in the little things and in the big things. I mean, look how much he has blessed Brad and his wife. And he has given us the children back, as well as our precious son. We do not deserve any of this."

"It's true. He has given us a lot. And he gave us each other and our marriage."

As good as things were at that point, I had no idea that God was about to bless our lives even more.

రెండెందె

In 1998, I returned to the church I had gone to on the bus as a young girl. The name had changed to New Hope International Church, but so many things were the same. Even many of the Sunday school teachers were still there, loving on people. In fact, the two "sisters" I remembered from childhood became very involved in ministry with me, showing up and staying late even on cold winter nights. They prayed such incredible prayers, and they inspired me to want to grow in the things of the Lord.

My youngest daughter's birth in April of 2001 reminded me how far I'd come from being an unfit mother. I'd become the mother of four amazing children. And my children were being raised in the church and in homes with two parents in them.

Shortly after my daughter's birth, my prayers to God were answered concerning my mom's relationship with him. I had been telling people about God's wonderful blessings in my life since I'd accepted a personal relationship with Jesus. I had invited my mom to church so many times. She never came, so I eventually stopped asking her.

When my youngest daughter was about 3 months old, my stepdad passed away, and my mother was devastated. She did not even want to get out of bed.

"Um, Tony? Is that my mom up there? It looks like her, but it can't be," I mused as I noticed two familiar-looking people in the front row at church.

"I think it is. It looks like her. And she looks like she is enjoying the music."

To my great delight, it was my mom and my aunt. My mom eventually began a relationship with God through Jesus and also found help for her own alcoholism. She never looked back.

I reconnected with my dad as well. It turned out that he had discovered Christ long before my mom and I did. After leaving our family, he had moved to Arizona, where he found sobriety. He prayed hard for my mom, my sisters and me to begin our own relationships with God. I fully believe his prayers are what led me to the Lord that December day in 1994.

I also worked a job I could never have dreamed of — selling custom windows in high-end homes. It struck me, however, that I could be standing in some of the most premier homes in the Bay area selling $30,000-plus in windows per home only a mile and a half from where I once had no belongings or place to call home, nothing but the clothes on my back. The time came for me to give something back after all I had been given.

ññññ

One of our pastors began a substance recovery ministry at New Hope. He talked to me about being a part of it, but the idea really intimidated me. Public speaking terrified me. I had dropped speech class three times in college.

Finally, I gave in and agreed to lead a group of women. I wondered if the pastor questioned himself for asking me to do it after I spent most of the first meeting with my head buried in my Bible barely able to look at anyone.

It got better after that initial meeting. Since then, I have met thousands of women through the recovery meetings held at New Hope. I believed that God touched lives through my work, but I also recognized how he taught me through them. And he continued to teach me about how faithful he is.

I still struggled with feeling capable of helping others. The old hurts from my childhood and turbulent young adult years kept me from giving things my all. I felt inadequate to be leading others. Tony and I struggled through some marriage issues as well. We were able to find help in a mentoring relationship with a pastor and his wife, but there were still some struggles and pain.

Then something amazing happened. Tony went away to a men's retreat and came back with such excitement for living for the Lord. He would not tell me much about it since it appeared to be something that truly needed to be experienced firsthand, but he encouraged me to go on a women's retreat. And I could not wait to go after seeing the change in him. He appeared more at peace inside and burned with enthusiasm for serving the Lord. I wanted what he had, so I signed up.

Attending my first Encounter weekend amazed me and started a whole new aspect of my spiritual journey. Through prayers and hearing others' testimonies, I received a deep healing regarding my past. I had dealt with many of my issues, but the Encounter experience brought up even more sore spots that had been hiding in my soul. So much pain was removed from my heart that weekend — pain that I did not even know still existed.

Such wonderful counselors prayed with me. They also asked me helpful questions, and they listened as I processed it all.

I realized during the Encounter weekend how deeply it affected me not to have a close relationship with my dad all those years. I did not have resentment toward him, but I had a deep sadness and broken heart that started to heal during the retreat.

And the years of little resentments that had built up in my marriage with Tony were lifted off of me that weekend. We had experienced difficulties and little disagreements that many married couples have, and I'd carried them with me. But that weekend, I felt set free from it all. I was able to see the many positives in my husband, and our marriage and my attitude changed. My marriage was brought to a whole new level of intimacy after that experience.

Along with the peace, I felt willing to participate on staff at a subsequent retreat. When I shared my testimony in front of several women, it scared me but ended up being a wonderful event. I felt I truly experienced the Holy Spirit moving in people as I prayed for them and felt a warmth come over them as the Holy Spirit filled them. I prayed for and saw women receive healing, both internally and externally. I have attended many women's Encounter weekends over the years and been touched by so many testimonies. I have shared my story many times as well.

Through Encounter, the recovery ministry and New Hope, I learned the importance of relationships and prayer. I learned how vital it is to have mentors in my life and people who will encourage me in my faith. And I continued to learn how important my relationship with the Lord is.

I learned this through reading my Bible and through prayer — listening to and talking with God. I hope when people look at my life, they see a life of prayer, which is the most important thing to me. I needed it when I was at the bottom with nothing, and it saved me. I needed it even when I had everything. I needed it for my relationship with Jesus to grow, and I needed it in order to do the work I believe God has called me to do.

❧❧❧

My oldest daughter surprised me one day when she said, "Mom, when I think back on growing up, I recall how you were always helping addicts. I remember all the meetings we would go to at church where you were talking with people and praying with them. I forget that you were an addict, too."

"Really? You don't remember how we had nothing? You don't remember all of the bad times?"

My precious daughter replied, "I guess I remember things after you found Jesus. I remember you sharing your faith. I remember you picking up ladies to make sure they could go to church. It did not matter how much they stank or how they were dressed. You talked to them about how God had changed your life and how he could change theirs."

This young lady helped me realize that I truly did have everything that mattered. While I still remembered what it was like to have nothing, she saw me with everything the Lord had given me. And she gave me even more by sharing that with me.

The woman who once had nothing truly did have everything. God truly brought me a long way. For me, that knowledge was priceless.

THE FINAL JUDGE
The Story of Gary
Written by Aimee Haywood

"I'll tell your wife, man."

Stan's threat stung like a snakebite.

What the hell is he talking about? My mind raced. *What did he have on me?*

"What do you mean?"

"Remember that girl last week?" I could hear his slimy grin spreading across his ugly face.

"Yeah, so what? What about her?" My voice snapped more harshly than I intended.

"I've got video."

His venom was working.

Video?

"Like hell you do." I spat my words back at him, hoping he couldn't hear my desperation.

He's playing me. He's got to be. He wouldn't do this to me. We're friends. That girl ... what we did ... what I couldn't do. Did he see everything? My mouth went sour.

"Look, Gary, I need money. You know this project I'm working on is drying up my funds. I have to hire more people this week so the guys will have some action to shoot."

"That's not my problem."

"Oh, but it is. I've got video of you and that girl. I'm

sure your wife would love to see it. See what you did. Oh, and how you couldn't even finish the deed." The last words oozed out of his mouth like slow poison.

That got me pissed. He *had* seen everything.

"Screw you!"

"Just give me those drugs your team confiscated last week. That should be enough to cover my expenses for a little while, officer." With that last word, he mocked me and my badge.

"You know I can't do that. Those drugs are scheduled to be destroyed."

"You'll be the one destroyed if you don't get me those drugs."

❧ ❧ ❧

I loved being a cop. I loved the authority that came with it. I had worked hard to become a police officer, falling in love with the job the day I went on my first ride-along.

I had earned my GED at a young age so that I could begin working in my dad's auto repair shop as a mechanic when I was 16. However, after that ride-along, I couldn't get my mind off police work. I set my mind in that direction, working at my dad's shop during the day and earning my certificate by going to night school for eight months. I became a reservist, a volunteer in full uniform, but I really wanted to be a police officer full time and couldn't find a full-time position without graduating from college or the police academy.

My dad had semi-retired from the shop, leaving me to run it on my own, but when I decided to go to the academy, he came back to take care of the shop in my absence. He wasn't happy about it. It was his hope that I'd carry on with the shop, making that my business and my career. When I told him I wanted to be a police officer and didn't want to run the shop anymore, he was really upset with me. I think he secretly hoped I wouldn't find a job and that I'd come back and follow in his footsteps. With my dad, there was no choice. What he said or what he wanted was the only choice. Being a police officer would let me make the decisions. I would hold the authority.

Despite my dad's obvious disappointment in me, I worked hard, and before I even graduated, I was hired full time by my local police department. I graduated fifth out of a class of 35. I would have earned more money as a mechanic, but police work had gotten into my blood. I was well-suited for it. I had the temperament, a type A personality, ego, strength, will and smarts. It was a perfect fit.

My dad was so heartbroken and angry that he sold his auto shop business. I didn't understand his reaction. He was the one who taught me how to be a man: Be strong, don't show emotion. I'd made my choice to be a cop, and I loved it, yet my father's heartbreak followed me from that day on, nagging, whispering that I was a disappointment.

かかか

"Hey, guys, can I talk to you all for a minute?" I gathered my friend Julie's kids into the family room and sat them all down on the couch.

I had met Julie through a mutual friend, and my babysitter lived just down the street from her. Our kids played together while we both were at our jobs, and that night, I wanted to talk to them all before Julie got home from work.

"What's up, Gary?" Her oldest, a teenager, looked at me, wondering what it was all about.

"I'll just get right to it. You know your mom and I have been good friends for a while now. You three are the most important people in her life, so I wanted to ask your permission to ask your mom out on a date."

The kids all smiled at each other and then smiled at me. Their grins granted me the approval I had been hoping for.

"All right. Well, let's wait for her to get home then."

The kids were excited, and so was I. They went back to what they'd been doing, and I grabbed the dozen roses I had bought already in hopes that the kids would say yes. I placed them on the dining room table, moving them back and forth just a little until they were positioned just right for her to see as soon as she walked in the door. It wasn't long before I heard her car pull up. The door opened, and her eyes went straight to the roses.

"Who are those for?" Her smile always had a way of making my own spread a little wider.

"They are for you."

I grinned back at her from behind the table.

"And what did I do to deserve such a beautiful gift?" She had stopped near the front door and was waiting for me to answer her.

"Well, I asked your kids if I could take you on a date, and they all said yes. So, these are in honor of our first date, whenever you choose that to be."

She looked at me, shocked and so happy. I could tell she was still thinking about her kids and what they had said.

"Okay." She nodded, showing me that beautiful smile. Our friendship had just gotten even friendlier.

❧❧❧

It was so dark I could barely see the gun on my hip. Sweat dripped into my eyes, stinging and making it hard to see. *Where was the guy?* I couldn't see anything in the darkness that spread out like a black curtain in front of me.

Click.

My head swung to the right to where the sound had come from, and then there were bullets, so many bullets. I dove behind my patrol car as the gunman's rounds poked holes in it. The sound was deafening.

Then it stopped. Dead quiet. I tried to breathe as I gripped my gun and raised it back up to my chest. Slowly, so very slowly, I raised myself up to peek back through the shattered windows of my car.

Nothing, again, I could see nothing. I tried to stop breathing so I could hear. Hear them breathe, hear them reloading or running. Nothing. Blood pounded so hard in every part of my body, I thought I was going to spring a leak.

Breathe. Get a grip, or you're gonna die out here!

Slowly, I stood and saw someone. He raised his gun at me, but I was faster and got off a shot. *Oh, God, no!*

My gun malfunctioned, and the bullet landed 10 feet in front of me. As I lifted my eyes to look up, I saw so many guns. Each of the barrels rising, in unison, pointing at me out of the darkness.

No, no, no!

I felt my body start to shake and shudder as the bullets came at me again. Shaking, shuddering … and then there were hands on me.

"Gary! Gary! Wake up!" My wife shook me with all she had.

I looked around. *Where was my patrol car? Why was my wife here?*

Tears rolled down her face.

"It was so real … I was getting shot at … what the …?" I still didn't quite know where I was.

For a second, I was sure I'd look down and see my uniform soaked in blood, but I was in shorts and a T-shirt, drenched in sweat.

"You had another nightmare." Julie looked scared and so very sad.

"I'm sorry, Julie. I didn't mean to scare you."

"It's okay, Gary. It's not your fault. Please get some help. They're getting worse."

"I know." I got up to change clothes. My wife was right, the nightmares were getting worse. I tried to take some deep breaths as I walked from the closet to the bathroom and turned on the cold water at the sink. I splashed my face and looked up at the shaking man staring back at me from the mirror. It was my face, but all I could hear was my dad's voice.

A real man doesn't cry, Gary. Men are strong. Emotions are for women. We don't need help. We help ourselves. Don't you dare try to talk to someone, Gary, and don't you dare cry.

Water ran down my face into the sink mimicking the tears I wished I could cry. *What the heck was happening to me? I'm a cop, on the drug force — and I AM A MAN.*

I stood up taller and stared down the guy looking back at me. I was the one people called when they needed help. There was no 911 for me. I turned from the sorry guy in the mirror and slammed the light off with my finger. I was a cop, a man. Feeling wasn't an option.

৵৵৵

"This is very concerning, Gary. With the neuropathy and now this disease, I really want to encourage you to retire from the force."

"But I'm a cop. I can work being sick." I looked at the doctor like he didn't know what he was talking about. *I'm one of the tough guys. I work out with weights every day. I'm a cop, on the SWAT team even. I take down drug dealers. I'm one of the invincible ones.*

"Gary, look. I know this is tough for you. But this disease attacks the nerves in your hands and feet. It's going to get worse with time and have a large impact on your ability to do your job. You will need frequent surgeries, and eventually, how you are able to walk will be affected. You'll need a walker and possibly a wheelchair. Please, consider retiring."

He rolled his chair back and stood, knowing I wasn't going to discuss it any further. Making a few notations in my chart, he put the folder down and walked back over to me, reaching out his hand.

"Thanks, doctor." I shook his hand and then left his office. *This disease won't beat me. It won't make me weak. I'll beat this.*

I tripped a little as I walked out to my car.

Did the disease just trip me, or was there a rock?

I looked back — no rock. Swallowing a jolt of fear, I got into my car and turned the key in the ignition. Checking my mirrors, I pulled into traffic.

I've got a job to do.

ॐॐॐ

I did not know that throughout my career, I was developing Post Traumatic Stress Disorder as a result of all the critical incidents I had experienced. I was a cop on the local force for 12 years, a member of the SWAT team for eight years and eventually moved to doing undercover work with the Department of Justice where I busted drug dealers and took countless amounts of drugs off the streets. I loved it. I loved the intensity.

My downfall started with depression. Then the nightmares began. All these got worse once I was diagnosed with Charcot-Marie-Tooth disease, a progressive muscle disease which caused the muscles, especially in my hands and feet, to atrophy. After about eight surgeries on my feet, the reality of this illness hit me. I began to lose interest in life. I stopped working out and would sit on the couch, eating and trying to zone out.

At this point, I was still able to work, despite all my mental and physical health problems. I was taking four to five over-the-counter sleeping pills a night to get to sleep, and within a year or two, I had graduated to stronger prescription sleeping pills. By then, I'd had 18 surgeries on my feet. I began limping and started to suffer bouts where I would lose my balance. Not a good thing when chasing bad guys.

A year or so later, I began losing feeling in my hands, which made it very hard to grip my gun and shoot. That's when the anxiety kicked in hard. I was in a hyper-vigilant state, constantly waiting and wondering if death was coming for me. I had never been a violent person, but without warning, anger burst out of me, scaring me and my family. I was out of control and unpredictable. I wanted to kill myself.

I pulled away from family and friends and began hoping that I'd get shot or hurt at work in the line of duty. I'd advanced quickly and with such success throughout my career that I cringed at the thought of supervisors putting me at a desk job because of all my health issues. If I couldn't do my job, I didn't want to live. Every day I hoped danger would find me and that an injury, not my disease, would decide my fate. I became reckless with myself. The line between right and wrong started to blur, when before I'd always been a cop who went by the book. I felt like I was dying, and everything I'd regarded as important didn't seem to matter so much anymore.

అఅఅ

"What did you just say?" I looked at my ex-wife, my daughter and back at the doctor.

"Your daughter's condition is severe, Gary." He paused, seeing if the news he had just given us would sink into my brain.

After a moment, I was able to speak. "So, now what?"

"Well, we can go a couple different ways with this. If one of the tumors on her liver was to burst, she could die within hours. Once those tumors rupture, it's basically like pouring poison right into her system, which would kill her. So we could do surgery, but the survival rate for surgery is only around 50 percent since we would have to remove 75 percent of the liver."

"Or?" I could feel my eyes widen, reaching out to him, wondering what the other option could possibly be.

"Or, we could do a biopsy, or we could do nothing and see if the tumors grow at all."

I looked at my sweet daughter. She and her mom looked like they were taking it all in, but me, I felt like someone had sucker punched me in the gut. *This is my fault. She has my DNA.*

"It's going to be okay, Dad. I survived illness when I was born, remember? I will do it again." Her smile almost made me cry like a baby right then and there. I looked away from her. I had to keep it together and be strong for her, not the other way around.

My daughter could die at any minute.

I watched her and her mom talking to each other and remembered how she had almost died as a baby. She needed a bone marrow transplant, and I was the only match. *Something must have gone wrong all those years before if she was having this problem now. With all my health problems, I probably did this to her.*

"We need to have some time to talk about this as a family, right?"

My daughter and ex-wife nodded at me.

We all left the office, and when I got in my car to return to work, I sobbed. Men weren't supposed to cry, but men weren't supposed to lose their daughters, either. The fear of my daughter dying overwhelmed me. It was just one more thing added to my plate.

Not my little girl. Not my little girl.

꙳꙳꙳

"Hey, man, you know that show on TV where they take kids into a jail and try to scare the bad behavior out of them? Well, this lady hired me to scare her son. He's been selling drugs. She wants us to intimidate him with a fake arrest. Can you help me out?"

Stan was a cop turned private investigator, and we went back a few years. He'd been forced to quit the force due to some inappropriate behavior. We'd lost touch, but then he made contact.

"What do you have in mind?" I hadn't gotten involved in Stan's P.I. work very much, just advised him here and there on surveillance or drug tactics. What he was talking about this time was something new.

"She knows her son has drugs. She wants us to buy the drugs from him, and then you can fake arrest him and threaten him with prosecution. She thinks it will scare him straight."

"I guess it would prevent the kid from getting arrested in the future and hopefully turn his life around, but I don't know."

"Talk to the mom, Gary. Just hear what she has to say?"

"Okay, fine. Give her my number."

After a few minutes, the mom convinced me. Her son was 19 years old and getting into a lifestyle she wanted to save him from. She wanted me involved because, being a decorated police officer, she trusted that I'd keep her son safe and make sure no one got hurt. I honestly thought I was doing a good thing. Wasn't it better to try and intervene in this kid's life before he ended up in the back of my cop car on true drug charges?

Stan and I worked out the details, and a few weeks later, the fake arrest had worked like a charm, and the mom was so appreciative to me.

When I talked to her afterward, all she could say was, "Thank you so much, Gary. You saved my son's life."

Little did I know that was the first in a series of compromising decisions that would change my life forever.

ॐॐॐ

I was walking, and the field seemed to go on for miles. *What was I doing here? How'd I get here?* I looked down, and I was in full uniform. *Why was I in this field?*

I turned around and saw nothing but more fields. I spun around, but no matter what direction I turned, the same view stretched out in front of me. I started to run. To where, I didn't know, but I had to move.

My foot brushed something as I ran, and I stopped and turned to see what it was.

A body. With no head.

I looked up to see where my backup was but found no one. I looked again. I remembered this body from one of my investigations. I closed my eyes, willing the image out of my head. I turned and began walking away, but I came upon another body.

A child this time.

A woman with a gunshot wound.

A tiny, helpless baby.

All dead. All faces I'd seen before.

All my investigations were strewn in that field in front of me. Reminding me of what I'd seen. The smell of death, all of them together — it was too much. I began to run again, unable to breathe, trying not to look, trying not to remember.

I was suffocating.

I tried for one last breath and grabbed for anything as I fell downward.

I awoke with my sheets wrapped around me.

Another nightmare.

Another night, looking at my wife who was begging me to get help.

"I'm taking more sleeping pills than I'm supposed to! I'm even taking pain pills during the day to take the edge off! What do you want from me?"

"You need to go talk to someone, Gary."

"I don't need anyone's help." I turned my back on her so I didn't have to see that same look on her face.

"Come on, Gary. Your work is taking its toll on you. It's understandable with all the stuff you've seen. It's not good for you to keep it all inside. It's okay to say you need help."

I spun on her then, seething. "I told you, I don't need help. I can do this on my own."

That really upset her.

"Oh, sure, you don't need help. The kids loved to be

around you as they were growing up. But now, when they come to visit us with their own families, they walk on eggshells because they don't know if nice Dad or angry Dad will be here!"

"Stop it, Julie!"

"And who's the guy who punched his fist through the wall of our brand-new remodeled bathroom the other day? That's not you, Gary! You are the sweetest, kindest, most loving man that I've ever known. You were the guy who used to sit and play tea parties with your little girl whenever she wanted! What is going on with you? Is there something else I need to know?"

No. Definitely not.

Get me those drugs, Gary, or you're going to be the one destroyed. I've got video, remember? Stan's words pricked like needles in my skull. I looked at my wife who had love in her eyes, still, after all my issues with the disease, all my work demands, all of it.

Julie, you don't even know that a couple weeks ago I stuck my handgun in my mouth after my shift. I wasn't going to come home that night or ever again. But I couldn't do it. There is so much I just can't do.

I looked again at my wife. "No, Julie, there isn't anything else. Go back to bed."

I walked into the bathroom and looked at myself in the mirror. The cop. The officer with 15 commendations on his record.

I didn't get all those accolades for being weak. What will the guys say if I walk into the office and they know I was just in with the psychologist? Yeah, right. A weak link, that's what they'll call me. It will be a desk job for me for sure.

"No!" A strong whisper spat out at the man looking back in the mirror.

"You are a man and a cop, and you can do this!"

I was a man with a failing body.

A man with a daughter who was due for another biopsy because the first one showed the tumor was still there, and it was growing.

A man who couldn't sleep without nightmares.

And I was a cop who stumbled when he walked.

A cop who had agreed to meet another woman so he could blame his wife for not doing it for him anymore.

I'm a well-known cop, and he's got me on video.

❧❧❧

"The court order for the destruction of property was signed yesterday." Stan nodded and smiled at me as we drove in silence toward the building where the drug task force evidence was held.

About halfway there, I looked up into the sky, thinking I saw a surveillance plane.

I looked over at Stan. He looked comfortable in the silence we were riding in, but I was starting to freak out. This was going to all come down on me. *I know better.*

He was getting what he wanted, and I wouldn't lose my wife. That was the deal. I was scared. A car slowed next to Stan's truck, and I wondered if they were undercover.

Stan turned into the parking lot, and we got out of the car. He walked right in with me. I signed out all the drugs that were to be destroyed. Everyone there knew me, so I signed my own name. Stan followed me into the evidence room. I grabbed what we were there for, and he just stood near me but was looking around.

Why did you bring him in here with you? This is really stupid! You are committing career suicide right now.

We walked out, and I looked up and remembered the surveillance cameras we'd just walked past. *Great, now they have me on video, too. I'm screwed.*

We got back in Stan's truck, and as we drove away, I heard a voice inside my head.

Stop this now, Gary.

I looked over at Stan, but I could tell he hadn't heard it.

I noticed a car in the side mirror that had been behind us for a while. *We're being followed.*

Again, that inner voice. *Stop this now, Gary.*

I heard the voice at least five times, telling me the same thing as we made our way to Stan's office, but I didn't listen.

Stan and I didn't say a word to each other the whole way, and he sold the drugs as soon as we got back. Then it hit me as he handed me my cut of the money. I felt sick. The deal was made, and the drugs were gone. Back on the streets.

What have I done? This isn't me. What have I done? How could I have done this? I'm a cop. I'm the good guy.

I've taken countless drugs off the street! What have I done? I don't want this money!

I drove straight home and put the money in my safe. I was sweating, wanting to explode. *What the hell was I doing?*

My bottle of sleeping pills sat next to the bed, and I immediately popped a few in my mouth. I didn't want to be awake anymore. I didn't want to think.

My eyes grew heavy, and everything got dark. *What have I done?*

ॐॐॐ

The phone rang.

"Gary?"

"Hey, boss, what's up?"

"I need you to go interview a girl. She's made a complaint about another officer, and she's under arrest over at their department."

"Sure, I'll go right now."

It was a cool California day, nice out, and the river running along the city was beautiful. I enjoyed the drive there. I locked my car and walked across the parking lot. As I opened the door and walked into the jail, I removed my gun as per protocol and locked it up like I was supposed to. As I turned around, two detectives from my agency were standing there.

"Gary, you are under arrest." The handcuffs wrapped around my wrists, and in that moment, I broke down and cried. I was caught.

A weight lifted off of me, and the stress I'd been carrying seemed to drift away as they read me my rights. *It's finally over.*

I agreed to tell them the whole story, but I left out that Stan had blackmailed me. I didn't want my infidelity coming out.

I sat there in handcuffs, more worried about losing and hurting my wife than I was for my freedom. They treated me well. They told me they heard me tell Stan I didn't want to do it, so that comforted me a bit. I explained the post-traumatic stress issues I was enduring, the nightmares and even the health issues and disease I had been diagnosed with years before. I told them about my precious daughter and my fears that she could die of her own health issues at any time.

They were respectful and professional. They allowed me to call my wife and ask her to go home so they could search the safe and find the money I'd taken from the sale of the drugs. It was all there, I never spent any of it. I cried as I called my wife.

"Julie."

"Hey, Gary. How's your day going?"

I could hear her smile, and tears poured down my face.

"I'm in jail."

"How are they treating you?"

I could tell by the sound of her voice she thought I was kidding.

"No, I've been arrested."

The phone was silent.

"Julie, I need you to go home, and let the deputies in when they get there. Show them where my safe is."

After I hung up with my wife, I was transported to the county jail where I knew a lot of the deputies. As I arrived, one of my bosses was waiting, and he opened the door and hugged me. I remember he was crying, too. I'd known him a long time, from my early days as a cop. He'd always tried to tell me about God. I'd tease him about loving Jesus. He was so sad for me and looked at me like he couldn't believe that something had brought me to this place. It wasn't like me.

That's the problem, though. It's not like first responders or military members to fall apart, to be depressed and not be able to push through. We were bred to be the unbreakable ones, and yet every day we willingly entered situations that exposed us to the worst of human nature. Our daily lives were filled with someone else's nightmare. Even among fellow officers, the support isn't always there. You're only a member if you've still got it together. It's wrong. And when we break, we don't get a dent, we shatter. And no one seems to know how to pick up the pieces.

I was booked into the jail. They fingerprinted me, took my DNA and mug shot. A few guys I knew came up to me and tried to comfort me, but I was ashamed and embarrassed and couldn't even talk to them. Being around all those guys I knew and had worked with for most of my career made me start to disassociate from the reality of the situation. I went from sobbing to not feeling a thing. The

TVs were on. From my cell, I could see my face plastered all over the news. *What had I done?*

❧❧❧

"Hey, John!" A woman approached our table and started hugging my dad.

"Hey, Mary, how are you?" They chatted for a couple of moments, and I gathered that this was the travel agent my dad had mentioned on past occasions. He had also mentioned she was really into church. I took a bite of my lunch while they caught up, but then she turned her attention to me. *She better not preach to me. I don't believe in God.*

"You must be Gary." She reached out to shake my hand and smiled at me like she was proud to meet my dad's son. I struggled to hold eye contact.

Why is she being so nice to me? I'm all over the news. Doesn't she know what I've done? Good grief, I'm out on bail right now!

"It's nice to meet you, Gary. You hang in there." She squeezed my hand, and her smile was so loving, I didn't quite know what to think. As quickly as she came, she was gone.

I looked at my dad and took another bite of my burger.

That was weird.

❧❧❧

"Hello?"

"Hi, is this Gary?" The voice sounded so chipper. *Who was this guy?*

"Yeah, it is. Who's this?" I turned the volume down on the show I was watching.

"My name's Jeff, and I'm the pastor at New Hope International Church here in town. Your dad's friend Mary asked me to call you. "

Are you serious? Like I want to hear anything about God or church right now. Give me a break.

I positioned my hand to hang up on the guy, but my mother's sweet face flashed through my mind telling me to be polite. She'd been my best friend and had passed on already. I wouldn't dare disappoint her.

Fine, Mom, I'll listen.

"Did you know my parents were from Germany, too?"

"No, I didn't." *That was random.*

Pastor Jeff went on to tell me about his church and that he did counseling if I thought I might want to meet with him. Honestly, I still wanted to hang up on the guy. *Come on!*

"Anyway, Gary, I'd love it if you'd come to church some Sunday and see what we are all about. How are you doing, anyway?"

Shame came upon me like a cold blanket.

"You probably know all about me already."

"No, I only know what I've heard through the media. But I'm sure there's much more to the real you than they've shared."

Who is this guy? Oh, well, he's already heard it all, I'm sure.

"Look, Jeff, I have no excuses for my actions. I'm really sorry for what I've done, but I can't do anything to change it now. The worst part about all of this is that my children and grandchildren thought I was this amazing guy, and now they are dealing with the knowledge of the darkness I was living in."

Was he there? The other side of the phone was silent.

"Gary, would you want to meet for lunch next week sometime?"

"Okay." *Why am I saying yes?*

"Great. I want to hear more about you and tell you more about myself. I hope you have a good night, despite all you're going through. Hey, can I pray for you before we hang up?"

"Sure."

"God, would you please be close to Gary in this season and reveal your purpose and plan to him? Amen."

"Amen."

"Gary, do you have a few more minutes?"

"Sure."

"I know I just prayed for you, but I'd like to pray with you again, if that's okay. See, all the darkness you said you were living in — all of that is a result of sin, our own and other people's. Sin separates us from God. God is love, and when we are separated from that love, life is so hard and so confusing. We've all sinned, Gary. We've all made mistakes and chosen things that have been our downfall.

Your sin is no different than mine. Sin is sin. But God wants to forgive you, Gary! Right now. Right in the middle of this mess. He wants you to have his peace. Would you like that?"

Why am I crying? Peace? Forgiveness? Of course I want that. Now?

"Gary, it's almost like there is a chalkboard in heaven with a list of every single sin you've committed your whole life. But tonight, God is taking out the eraser, and he's going to wipe them all away. Can I pray with you now?"

"Yeah, if you want to." I honestly still just wanted to hang up the phone. I didn't know what to say. I was sitting there feeling sorry for myself, and suddenly there's this guy on the phone praying for me?

"God, we admit we are sinners and that there is nothing we can do to earn your love or find our way to you on our own. We understand that because you love us, you sent your son to take our place. He took the eternal punishment that we had rightfully earned with our sin. We believe that Jesus is our Savior and our Lord and our only way back to you. Thank you, God, that nothing we have done or will do can separate us from you ever again when only Jesus is our judge. Thank you for your love, God. Amen."

"Amen."

"I'm looking forward to getting together, Gary. Goodnight."

"Thank you. Goodnight."

I couldn't control the tears that started coming. My

wife was at my side all of a sudden, and I tried to explain to her what happened and what Jeff had said.

"I feel funny, Julie."

"What do you mean?"

"I don't know, I feel calm. I feel like I'm lighter. Like someone just took a really heavy jacket off my shoulders."

"That's great." She smiled and hugged me. She seemed to understand more than I did.

"I'm having lunch with him on Wednesday, and I think I'm going to check out his church on Sunday."

She nodded, tears filling her eyes, too, as she hugged me again.

かかか

I had lunch with Jeff, and we began meeting every Wednesday. He would give me stuff to read in the Bible, and we'd talk about what I'd read over a cup of coffee. He also prayed with me about my daughter and what her future held. We always met at the church because I hated being out in public where people could look at me and judge me, knowing what I did because of all the media coverage.

I'd disappointed myself, my family, my fellow officers and the community. It was just too hard. I liked meeting at the church, where it felt safe.

"Gary, let's go to a restaurant today." Jeff smiled and spoke like it was decided.

"What if someone recognizes me?" I was terrified. Jeff

and the people from the church looked at me with love and support and felt like family. The general public looked at me like I was a monster walking in their midst.

"It's okay, Gary. I want to be with you when that happens. Let's go."

We arrived at the restaurant, and I didn't see anyone I recognized. I didn't mind the general public, but I most feared seeing other law enforcement members. I had totally betrayed them. I was also hurt, though, because since everything happened, those who I thought were my close friends hadn't even called to check on me. It hurt.

We settled in and were halfway through our meal when I saw them.

"Gary? Are you all right? You're white as a ghost!" Jeff turned and saw the two officers in uniform looking back at me.

"I gotta get out of here." I was sweating. My anxiety went through the roof. Jeff slid his keys across the table.

"I'll pay and meet ya in the truck."

I felt like I was running out of there. I fumbled as I tried to unlock his truck door and jump in. I was trying to breathe, in and out, and it felt like forever until Jeff jumped in beside me.

"They asked about you, ya know? Wanted to know how you were doing."

"What?" I was stunned.

"Yeah, one of them told me to tell you that there is redemption for all of us, including you."

I hadn't cried for most of my life, but in those days, I

couldn't stop crying. Tears fell again as I looked at Jeff and nodded.

"Thank you."

"Let's get out of here."

෨෨෨

"I'm sorry, what did you just say?" I was back at the doctor with my daughter and my ex-wife. We'd decided that we had waited long enough, and it was time for her to have the biopsy done.

"Like I said, I can't explain this. This is the film from before, and this is the film from now. She is tumor free."

"Her liver is fine?" I stared at the doctor. *Could this be real?*

"Yes. It's a miracle. There is nothing wrong with her. She's been healed."

෨෨෨

I figured God must have known I was still on the fence about whether to believe in him or not. I had felt different after Jeff prayed with me on the phone, but I still didn't know if I could believe that God loved me, despite everything. Life still felt overwhelming. There was a good chance that I was going to go to prison. I was out on bail, but a trial was going to happen. Would I be sent to jail and be taken from my family?

When I sat there in the doctor's office with my daughter and realized that she was in perfect health, I accepted that God had demonstrated something to me. He must have known I needed to see how big he was. I'd needed him to show off. My little girl's death sentence had been torn up, and she was going to live.

I sat at home that night not knowing what to think. There was no explanation, but the truth was she would live. I wanted to live, too. No matter what else happened, I finally believed in him.

❧ ❧ ❧

"Grandpa, why did you have to go away?"

My grandson's voice broke my heart as I listened to his question during a call from prison.

"Well, Grandpa took something from work that he shouldn't have, and so he had to go to jail."

"I took a flashlight from a store the other day, Grandpa. But Mom caught me and made me go back in and tell them what I did."

"That's good. We should always say when we've done something wrong, Jason." I wept silently as I listened to this little boy I loved with all my heart.

"Yeah, I'm really glad I didn't have to go to jail, too. But I miss you."

"I miss you, too, Jason. Grandpa loves you, and I'm proud of you for admitting you did something wrong, even if it was hard."

"You, too, Grandpa. I love you. Goodnight."

I hung up the receiver and went back to my cell. I might have been serving my sentence in prison, but I recognized that God helped me escape darkness and depression and bring me back to him. I was captive behind bars, but I decided to use my time well, studying to get my master's degree in theology and counseling. I intimately understood the depression, the suicidal thoughts and the pain that many first responders and military veterans silently struggled with.

Through horrible circumstances, I learned that the world doesn't know what to do when those they regard as heroes fall. Thankfully, though, I believe in a God who does. I believe that he was the one whispering to me that day on the way to the evidence room. I just didn't listen.

I used to think I was better than those I always got called out to help. Life was black and white, and pain was another person's issue. I finally realized that the world is full of broken, messed-up people, and I am just one of the many.

When the doors of my prison cell open for the last time, I can't wait to get out of here and help others who feel trapped like I did all those years. There is help. Asking for it is not weakness, it is strength. And when real men do cry, all it shows is that they're alive.

Despite being apart, my family and I have gotten closer than we've ever been. My entire family goes to church now, whereas before, I don't think most of us knew who God really was. It took more effort, but I figured out how to teach lessons to my children and grandchildren from prison, and my wife made sure to keep me aware of everything going on in their lives.

My choices had consequences, and I'm paying for my mistakes. I wish I'd known how to be honest about myself and my pain earlier when the hurts all started to surface. It would have made all the difference. And when that little voice told me to stop, I really wish I had listened.

No matter what happens, I believe that God will be my final judge, that he has already given me his sentence and that with him, there is hope.

Even from behind bars, God helped me become freer than I'd ever been.

CONCLUSION

When I came to this church in 1975 as a teenager, our family was a wreck. Alcoholism, unfaithfulness, anger, mental illness and abuse had almost destroyed us. I discovered hope beyond the wreckage, and 20 years later, I became the senior pastor. Over the past four decades, I have witnessed hundreds of people who discovered hope beyond their personal wreckage.

A few years ago, my wife, Missy, had a dream to write a book to share the amazing stories of some of the fascinating people at NHIC. This book is a dream come true. Unfortunately, we could only share seven stories. As I read through the accounts in this book, my heart is filled with gratitude for the many lives that have been changed because of the loving, accepting and caring atmosphere in our congregation. Rather than being content with our past and current stories of HOPE, we are spurred to believe that many more can occur.

Every time we see another changed life, it increases our awareness that God really loves people and he is actively seeking to change lives. Think about it: How did you get this book? We believe you read this book because God brought it to you seeking to reveal his love to you. Whether you're a man or a woman, a biker or a nurse, blue collar or no collar, a parent or a student, gang member or police officer, we believe God came to save you. He came to save all of us from the hellish pain we've accepted as normal and to offer real joy, hope and lasting peace through a personal relationship with his one and only son, Jesus Christ.

You probably have honest questions about how this radical change is possible. All of us at New Hope International Church extend our sincere and warm invitation for you to come and check out our church family. Freely ask questions, examine our statements, see if we're "*for real*" and, if you choose, journey with us at whatever pace you are comfortable. You will find that we are far from perfect. Our scars and sometimes open wounds are still healing, but we just want you to know God is still completing the process of authentic life change in us. We still make mistakes in our journey, like everyone will. Therefore, we acknowledge our continued need for each other's forgiveness and support.

If you are unable to be with us, yet you intuitively sense you would really like to experience such a life change, here are some basic thoughts to consider. If you choose, at the end of this conclusion, you can pray the suggested prayer. If your prayer genuinely comes from your heart, you will experience the beginning stages of authentic life change, similar to those you have read about.

How does this change occur?

Recognize that what you're doing isn't working. Accept the fact that Jesus desires to forgive you for your bad decisions and selfish motives. Realize that without this forgiveness, you will continue a life separated from God and his amazing love. In the Bible, the book of Romans, chapter 6, verse 23 tells us that the result of sin (*seeking our way rather than God's way*) is death (*eternal separation from God*), but the gift that God freely gives is everlasting life found in Jesus Christ.

Believe in your heart that God passionately loves you and wants to give you a new heart. Ezekiel 11:19 reads, "I will give them singleness of heart and put a new spirit within them. I will take away their stony, stubborn heart and give them a tender, responsive heart" (NLT).

Believe in your heart that "if you confess with your mouth that Jesus is Lord and believe in your heart that God raised him from the dead, you will be saved" (Romans 10:9 NLT).

Believe in your heart that because Jesus paid for your failure and wrong motives, and because you asked him to forgive you, he has filled your new heart with his life in such a way that he transforms you from the inside out. Second Corinthians 5:17 reads, "When someone becomes a Christian, he becomes a brand new person inside. He is not the same anymore. A new life has begun!"

Why not pray right now? Pray this prayer from your heart:

Lord Jesus, if I've learned one thing in my journey, it's that you are God and I am not. My choices have not resulted in the happiness I hoped they would bring. Not only have I experienced pain, I've also caused it. I know I am separated from you, but I want that to change. I am sorry for the choices I've made that have hurt myself, others and denied you. I believe your death paid for my sins, and you are now alive to change me from the inside out. Would you please do that now? I ask you to come and live in me so that I can sense you are here with me. Thank you for hearing and changing me. Now please help me know when you are talking to me, so I can cooperate with your efforts to change me. Amen.

Concord's unfolding story of God's love is still being written … and we believe your name is in it. We sincerely hope to see you this Sunday at 9 or 11 a.m.

Pastors Jeff and Missy Kenney
New Hope International Church
Concord, California
www.getnewhope.net

We would love for you to join us at New Hope International Church!

We meet Sunday mornings at 9 and 11 a.m. at 2120 Olivera Court, Concord, CA 94520.

Contact Information
Phone: 925.682.5918
Web site: www.getnewhope.net
Email: wegothope@yahoo.com

For more information on reaching your city with
stories from your church, go to
www.testimonybooks.com.

GOOD CATCH
PUBLISHING